**At Issue**

# Are Textbooks Biased?

# Other Books in the At Issue Series:

Are Americans Overmedicated?

Are Newspapers Becoming Extinct?

Are Social Networking Sites Harmful?

Book Banning

Cell Phones and Driving

Drunk Driving

The Ethics of Capital Punishment

Food Safety

How Can the Poor Be Helped?

Is Socialism Harmful?

Media Bias

Should Music Lyrics Be Censored?

Should Religious Symbols Be Allowed on Public Land?

Should There Be An International Climate Treaty?

Weapons of War

What Is the Impact of E-Waste

# At Issue

# Are Textbooks Biased?

*Noah Berlatsky, Book Editor*

**GREENHAVEN PRESS**
*A part of Gale, Cengage Learning*

WILLOW INTERNATIONAL LIBRARY

GALE
CENGAGE Learning

Detroit • New York • San Francisco • New Haven, Conn • Waterville, Maine • London

Elizabeth Des Chenes, *Managing Editor*

© 2012 Greenhaven Press, a part of Gale, Cengage Learning.

Gale and Greenhaven Press are registered trademarks used herein under license.

*For more information, contact:*
Greenhaven Press
27500 Drake Rd.
Farmington Hills, MI 48331-3535
Or you can visit our Internet site at gale.cengage.com

For product information and technology assistance, contact us at

Gale Customer Support, 1-800-877-4253
For permission to use material from this text or product, submit all requests online at www.cengage.com/permissions

Further permissions questions can be emailed to permissionrequest@cengage.com

Articles in Greenhaven Press anthologies are often edited for length to meet page requirements. In addition, original titles of these works are changed to clearly present the main thesis and to explicitly indicate the author's opinion. Every effort is made to ensure that Greenhaven Press accurately reflects the original intent of the authors. Every effort has been made to trace the owners of copyrighted material.

Cover Image copyright © Todd Davidson/Illustration Works/Corbis.

**LIBRARY OF CONGRESS CATALOGING-IN-PUBLICATION DATA**

Are Textbooks Biased? / Noah Berlatsky, book editor.
    p. cm. -- (At issue)
  Includes bibliographical references and index.
  ISBN 978-0-7377-5550-3 (hardcover) -- ISBN 978-0-7377-5551-0 (pbk.)
  1. Textbooks--United States. 2. Censorship--United States. I. Berlatsky, Noah. II. Title. III. Series.
  LB3047.A74 2012
  371.3'2--dc23

                                     2011026842

Printed in the United States of America
1 2 3 4 5 6 7 15 14 13 12 11

# Contents

Introduction                                                    7

1. Censorship From the Left and Right                          10
   Distorts Textbooks
   *Anne C. Westwater*

2. Conservatives Are Attempting to Insert                      23
   Bias Into Textbooks
   *Mariah Blake*

3. Textbooks Display a Liberal Bias                            35
   and an Anti-American Slant
   *Marcia Segelstein*

4. Textbooks Are Biased in Favor of                            41
   American Ethnocentrism
   *James W. Loewen*

5. Textbooks Are Biased Against Women                          48
   in America
   *Rae Lesser Blumberg*

6. Textbooks Are Biased In Favor of Islam                      58
   *Gary A. Tobin and Dennis R. Ybarra*

7. Textbooks Are Not Biased in Favor                           66
   of Islam
   *Susan Douglass*

8. Textbooks Are Biased in Favor                               70
   of Evolution
   *Casey Luskin*

9. Textbooks That Teach Evolution                              74
   Are Not Biased
   *Glenn Branch*

10. The Abstinence-Only Sex Education                    78
    Curriculum Is Biased and Dangerous
    *Eric Alterman and George Zornick*

11. The Abstinence-Only Sex Education                    85
    Curriculum Is Effective
    *Christine Kim and Robert Rector*

12. Textbook Content Should Be Controlled                98
    By Experts
    *Marie Landau*

13. Parents Should Have More Choice                     102
    In Curriculum Content
    *Andrew J. Coulson*

14. Textbook Biases Are Indicative of Broader           106
    Educational Problems
    *Sara Mayeux*

Organizations to Contact                                114

Bibliography                                            118

Index                                                   123

# Introduction

One of the biggest controversies over textbooks in recent US history occurred in 1974, in Kanawha County, West Virginia. In April of that year, due in part to funding pressure, "the five-member Kanawha County Board of Education voted unanimously to adopt 325 recommended texts and supplementary books in language arts," according to an article on the controversy in the online *West Virginia Encyclopedia*.

However, soon after the vote, school-board member Alice Moore had second thoughts about the board's decision. In particular, Moore was concerned that *The Autobiography of Malcolm X*, which was part of the approved curriculum, included pro-Muslim and anti-Christian statements. She publicly attacked the approved books as un-Christian and un-American, and was joined in her position by several local ministers as well. One of them, Reverend Lewis Harrah, explained their position regarding the selected textbooks in the following statement to a National Education Association panel:

> The standards and articles of faith of our church rest completely in our belief that the Bible is the absolute, infallible Word of God. We do not intend to compromise our beliefs, nor do we intend to agree to go to Hell, even if the majority of the people vote to do so. This is not a situation where opposing views can be reconciled.[1]

Others addressed the conflict differently. For example, in a demonstration led by Rev. Marvin Horan that included 8,000 people, Horan urged people to keep their children out of school. According to an essay on *American RadioWorks* titled "The Great Textbook War," the day after Horan' demonstration, "a large number of students failed to show up. Disputes

---

1. National Education Association, Teachers Rights Division, Inquiry Report, *Kanawha County West Virginia: A Textbook Study in Cultural Conflict*, Washington, DC: National Education Association, 1975.

raged over the numbers. Anti-textbook forces said as many as half the school children in Kanawha County were kept home to protest the books. The school system reported that about 20 percent of students were absent on that first day. Textbook supporters said many students were held out for their own safety, not over objections to the books."

Protestors formed picket lines around local businesses, shutting many of them down. On September 4, 1974, coal miners went on strike to protest the books. The school board pulled the textbooks temporarily, but this exacerbated tensions on both sides even further. The situation escalated and an anti-textbook demonstrator was shot and wounded, and the shooter beaten severely. As the national media began to take notice, the Ku Klux Klan (KKK), a white supremacist group, sent leaders to the region to support the anti-textbook cause. Explosives were thrown into schools; dynamite was detonated near the board of education office.

On November 8, the textbooks were reinstated, but the protests and violence continued. "In one incident, snipers fired on state police cruisers that were accompanying school buses. In another, a protestor fired a shotgun at a school bus," according to *American RadioWorks*.

The conflict had a chilling effect on teachers, according to Richard Clendenin, president of the Kanawha County Association of Teachers of English, as reported in the National Education Association report. In a statement, Clendenin explained how the teachers felt:

> Since the advent of this controversy, the English teachers and the subjects they teach have received the brunt of much of the ridicule stemming from the adoption of the English Language Arts texts. We have been called Communists, n-----lovers, professional elitists and pseudo-intellectuals. . . . Many feel threatened and have been threatened in the outlying areas of the country. Many feel they are going to be attacked if they say the wrong thing in the classroom.[2]

2. Ibid.

The West Virginia textbook wars eventually ended and the textbooks remained part of the curriculum. And although Rev. Marvin Horan was tried and convicted of plotting to bomb two schools, the end result was not really a victory for the pro-textbook forces. On the contrary, Alice Moore, the school board member who had initiated the controversy, won approval for new guidelines for textbook adoption. According to the *West Virginia Encyclopedia*, "These guidelines barred texts that pry into home life; teach racial hatred; undermine religious, ethnic, or racial groups; encourage sedition; insult patriotism; teach that an alien form of government is acceptable; use the name of God in vain; or use offensive language." In addition, principals in the county were given the power to reject individual books. As a result, books that were considered the most controversial were not allowed in schools in the areas that objected most stridently, according to *American Radioworks*.

The textbook conflict in Kanawha County is just one example of many such battles over what American schoolchildren should be taught. In school districts all over the country, arguments have arisen over the contents of textbooks, with many debates centering on the issue of bias. In *At Issue: Are Textbooks Biased?* the authors present a diverse array of views on the question of accuracy and balance in classroom materials.

# 1

# Censorship from the Left and Right Distorts Textbooks

*Anne C. Westwater*

*Anne C. Westwater is a retired teacher of biology, earth science, and environmental science.*

*Textbooks are censored in order to meet the demands of those on the right and those on the left. Thus all controversial language and subjects—and many that are not particularly controversial—are kept out of textbooks. As a result, textbooks. are bland and deceptive; they present an unreal world without conflict, ideas, or interest. Textbook selection processes should be taken away from states and given to individual teachers. In addition, the processes that result in textbook censorship—including bias and sensitivity review panels—should be made public. If these changes are implemented, the pressure groups that impose censorship on textbooks will have far less power.*

Are you an educator? An educator-in-training? A member of a school board? A parent of a public-school student? A journalist who reports on educational affairs? A citizen who wonders why public education in this country has degenerated so badly? If you are any of those, I strongly suggest that you read Diane Ravitch's book *The Language Police* just as soon as you can get a copy of it. . . .

## Pervasive Censorship

The subject of *The Language Police* is censorship—a formal, pervasive system of censorship that warps the content of schoolbooks, state-sponsored tests, and other educational products until they have little connection with the real world. The information in *The Language Police* helps to explain why many students find their curricula and schoolbooks irrelevant and uninteresting, and it explains, in part, the disturbing spectacle that we see in many parts of the United States: While the cost of public education rises higher and higher, the quality of that education continues to be low. What you will read in *The Language Police* should infuriate you, and it may even make you want to scream. Go ahead! I did.

Why has *The Language Police* upset me so? Because Ravitch has laid bare "an elaborate, well-established protocol of beneficent censorship, quietly endorsed and broadly implemented by textbook publishers, testing agencies, professional associations, states, and the federal government" that steadily and stealthily reduces schoolbooks to packages of pabulum. The arbiters of political correctness on the left have joined with the fundamentalist guardians of morality on the right to foster a censorship apparatus that serves the political and social agendas of both, scorns the interests of students, and ensures that students will not be exposed to anything that might bother anyone, anywhere, for any reason.

Ravitch has given the name "the language police" to the pressure groups that exploit this apparatus and the censors that run it.

---

*The language police have created a grossly fictitious, extremely odd world of their own, and they are foisting that world onto students as if it were real.*

---

## Bias and Sensitivity Review Panels

Diane Ravitch, a distinguished historian of education, first encountered the language police while she was a member of a nonpartisan federal education agency called the National As-

11

sessment Governing Board (NAGB). She was nominated to that agency by President Bill Clinton and began her service in 1998.

The NAGB had been charged with creating questions for use in a broad program of national educational testing, and Ravitch was assigned to a committee whose job was to choose written passages that would test 4th-graders' reading and reading-comprehension skills. The committee did its work, but some passages which the committee approved were later excluded by the corporation that had been hired to put the 4th-grade reading tests together. Why? Because those passages had been condemned by the corporation's "bias and sensitivity review" panel. When Ravitch and the other members of the NAGB's 4th-grade committee obtained copies of the "bias and sensitivity review" panel's judgments, they saw things that astounded them. For example:

- The panel had axed two passages that dealt with peanuts. One passage had failed to survive scrutiny because it stated that peanuts made a nutritious snack; this, the panel declared, displayed bias against people in whom peanuts produce allergic reactions. The second passage, which summarized the peanut's history, had been dumped because it contained the term *African slaves* and because it told that Spanish and Portuguese explorers had defeated indigenous tribes.

- The panel had rejected a story about quilting, as practiced by girls and women on the American frontier in the 1800s, because quilting made females seem "soft" and "submissive."

- The panel had rejected a story which told how a rotting stump sheltered a succession of organisms, and which compared the decaying stump to an apartment house. This was unacceptable, the panel said, because it denigrated apartment houses and the people who lived in them!

- The panel had tossed out a passage about owls, because Navajos regard owls as tabu.

- The panel had expelled a story about a blind man who allegedly had hiked to the top of Mount McKinley, because the story was offensive on two counts. First, it displayed "regional bias"; this meant that the story, because of its distinctive setting, could be understood more easily by a child who dwelt on a mountain than by a child who didn't. Second, the story suggested that blindness was a disadvantage in coping with difficult, dangerous situations. This suggestion was impermissible because, in the world of the language police, neither blindness nor any other disability is a handicap.

- The panel had torpedoed a passage that dealt with dolphins, because dolphins live in the sea. The sea is another distinctive setting, so this story, too, was damned for "regional bias."

These cases, along with others like them, provided Ravitch's introduction to "bias and sensitivity review."

## A Grossly Fictitious World

I have been a teacher for more than 25 years. During all this time I have known that schoolbook-writers sanitize their products by avoiding certain words (such as *evolution*) and certain concepts (such as cannibalism, infanticide, or the religious beliefs held by Mormons); and lately I have become increasingly aware of how schoolbook-writers use lumpy, politically correct euphemisms in place of real English—*enslaved African Americans* in place of *black slaves*, for example. But not until I read *The Language Police* did I recognize the extent, the complexity and the rigor of the censorship system that degrades and impoverishes both the literary characteristics and the conceptual features of the books that students read in our schools.

The language police have created a grossly fictitious, extremely odd world of their own, and they are foisting that world onto students as if it were real.

In that odd world, everybody is normal, and nobody is old or elderly, because the language police have abolished the words *abnormal, old* and *elderly*. That odd world doesn't have any lumberjacks or gypsies or pagans or tribesmen or jungles, nor does it have a Middle East, because the language police have banned the terms *lumberjack, gypsy, pagan, tribesman, jungle* and *Middle East*. Likewise, it doesn't have any cowboys, draftsmen, dwarfs, diabetics, fanatics, hordes, horsemen, huts, illegal aliens, lunatics, masterpieces, midgets, snow balls, snowmen, waitresses or yachts. Indeed, it lacks thousands of things that are common in the real world and that appear every day in the real world's books, news media, and entertainment media.

"Some of this censorship is trivial," Ravitch writes, "some is ludicrous, and some is breathtaking in its power to dumb down what children learn in school."

When this system of censorship began to take shape, it was justified as a way to ensure that educational materials would be free of language and images that were "racist" or "sexist" or "elitist," whatever those terms may have meant. Since then, it has expanded to include bizarre systems of "sensitivity reviews" and "bias reviews" that embody unfathomable notions of what is "racist" or "sexist," along with a deranged concept of what is "elitist." No matter how your dictionary may define *elitist* or *elitism*, the language police have decided that *elitism* simply means material wealth, and that students must not see words or phrases—such as *yacht, polo, junk bonds, cotillion* or *regatta*—that are associated with the lifestyles of people who are rich. This is part of a larger effort to protect students from the "bias" that they would experience if they had to read about people who were different from themselves, or about things that weren't already familiar to them.

## Controlling Both Content and Vocabulary

As she learned more about the censorship system, Ravitch found that it governs not only the composing of tests but also the creation of schoolbooks. Moreover, the censoring of schoolbooks extends far beyond the banning of individual words and phrases. The censors have also outlawed myriad topics, images, and modes of presentation that they don't like, and they thus have gained control of content as well as vocabulary.

In *The Language Police*, Ravitch focuses on how censorship affects "readers" (books that are used in teaching youngsters how to read), literature anthologies, and history books.

The language police force the writers and editors of textbooks to avoid so many topics that the books are disconnected from the real world that students experience every day. The characters in schoolbook stories must not speak in dialects, ponder suicide, face fire hazards or have poor eating habits. No one is allowed to encounter scorpions, rats, roaches or any other animals that anyone, anywhere might regard as scary or dirty. No one ever exhibits disrespectful or illegal behavior. No one steals, smokes, drinks alcohol, gets into fights, or tells lies. No one talks about politics, religion, unemployment, weapons, violence, child abuse, or animal abuse. Real life doesn't intrude.

---

*Schoolbooks that conform to rules devised by the language police are bland, boring, replete with simplistic social, political and religious messages, and stripped of nearly everything that is colorful or that might provoke thought.*

---

There is much more. Stories involving fantasy or magic are forbidden. So are stories set in prehistoric times, because such stories suggest organic evolution. So are stories about birthday parties, which are outlawed because some people don't celebrate birthdays. And even if a birthday party crept into a story, no one at the party would be able to eat the cake: Foods such as cake, candy, French fries or soft drinks have been prohibited in favor of more healthful items like dried beans, yogurt, and whole-grain breads. Real life doesn't intrude.

Do you want more? Then consider some of the rules that the publishers follow to generate "representational fairness." Schoolbooks and other instructional materials must have equal numbers of males and females in illustrations and in written passages, and the males and females must perform the same or comparable activities. (In answer to your question: Yes, pressure groups do take inventory!) Women cannot be portrayed as stay-at-home mothers and caregivers, because such images are "gender stereotypes" that anger radical feminists. Old persons must not be portrayed as feeble or sick, because those are "age stereotypes." Nor can old folks engage in sedentary activities like fishing or baking; they must go jogging or repair roofs. Real life doesn't intrude.

There are rules that govern English usage, too. The feminine pronouns must not be used for referring to countries or ships, and humans must not be compared to other animals. (The boxer Mohammed Ali said that he could float like a butterfly and sting like a bee, but his famous boast couldn't appear in a schoolbook.) And any animal other than a human must be designated by the pronoun *it*, not by *he* or *she*. (Imagine trying to read a description of the courtship ritual of a pair of birds, with both the male and the female designated as "it." How could you know who was doing what to whom?)

Schoolbooks that conform to rules devised by the language police are bland, boring, replete with simplistic social, political and religious messages, and stripped of nearly everything that is colorful or that might provoke thought. All that remains is insipid pap. In the real world, Ravitch reminds us, students are exposed continually to powerful stimuli supplied by television, pop music, films, videos and the Internet, as well as the unconstrained language of their peers—but their sterilized schoolbooks are unable to stimulate anyone. It's no wonder that students show indifference and contempt toward the materials that are presented to them at school!

## How Publishers Censor Themselves

Most of the censorship practiced by publishers of educational materials is self-censorship, originated and administered by the publishers themselves. Some state agencies (such as the California State Department of Education) issue regulations that tell publishers how to sterilize their products and how to make those products conform to state-approved religious, social and political ideologies, but such regulations seem less important than the publishers' own censorship rules and censorship mechanisms.

Each schoolbook company keeps track of the demands made by pressure groups, supplements them with guesses about demands that groups may make in the future, and supplements them further with lists of words, phrases, usages, and concepts that have been attacked during schoolbook-adoption proceedings conducted by state governments. The items compiled during this process are organized into a set of guidelines for sanitizing what students will read, and the guidelines are used by the company's internal censors, who have been trained to delete or replace or revise anything that might be considered controversial. The goal of this self-censorship, this "pre-emptive capitulation," is to ensure that the company's books will not contain anything that might upset any student, disturb any parent, cause any trouble during any state's adoption process, or result in the loss of a sale. In other words, the goal of self-censorship is to protect the company's bottom line.

## From Left and Right

The pressure groups that terrify publishers, and drive them to engage in self-censorship, come from both the political right and the political left. What they have in common is this: They all believe that reality follows language. They all imagine that if they can stop people from seeing certain words or reading about certain concepts, they can stop people from thinking about or committing the acts that the words or concepts imply.

Ravitch tells that publishers generally have allowed right-wing pressure groups to control topics and content. These groups want schoolbooks to reflect their idealized vision of the past—an imaginary past in which all families were happy because they had a strong father, a nurturing mother, obedient children, and a firm religious foundation. Crime, violence, divorce, abortion, and homosexuality did not exist in that fantasy-past, so they must never appear in any schoolbooks.

Leftist pressure groups generally hold the power to control vocabulary, to outlaw words and phrases, and to choose the words, phrases, and modes of usage that will be deemed politically correct. The demands made by leftist groups revolve around their vision of a utopian future in which egalitarianism prevails in all social relationships. Ravitch writes:

> In this vision, there is no dominant group, no dominant father, no dominant race, and no dominant gender. In this world, youth is not an advantage, and disability is not a disadvantage. There is no hierarchy of better or worse; all nations and all cultures are of equal accomplishment and value. All individuals and groups share equally in the roles, rewards and activities of society. In this world to be, everyone has high self-esteem, eats healthful foods, exercises, and enjoys being different. . . . [Pressure groups on the left] want children to read only descriptions of the world as they think it should be in order to help bring this new world into being.

Ravitch obtained sets of self-censorship guidelines that had been devised by some schoolbook companies, by some state agencies, and by such organizations as the Association of Education Publishers and the Educational Testing Service. From these, she generated an appendix, titled "Glossary of Banned Words, Usages, Stereotypes and Topics," which covers pages 183 through 218 of the paperback edition of *The Language Police*. Read it. And be prepared to feel your jaw drop and your stomach turn.

As it happens, the lists of words and phrases that writers of instructional materials must avoid include some personal favorites of mine: *fisherman, fireman, brotherhood, mankind, bookworm, actress, devil, Eskimo, Sioux, fellowship, senile, freshman, coed, tomboy, soul food, snow cone, Navajo* and *waitress*. If I were to write my autobiography, I would use about a dozen of those words in describing myself at various stages of my life, or in describing events that I experienced. Of course, my autobiography would never be chosen by a schoolbook company for use in an anthology.

Or maybe it would. Schoolbook companies regularly (and often secretly) sanitize stories and essays that they want to include in anthologies, so maybe some company would take my autobiography, delete any banned words, and replace them with words that the language police permit to be used.

## Distorting Literature and History

In the category of censorship that is "breathtaking" in its power to deprive children of opportunities to learn, the long campaign to outlaw Mark Twain's *Adventures of Huckleberry Finn* is especially disturbing. Ravitch reminds us that since the 1950s, this book has been the leading target of leftists, who revile Twain's repeated use of the word *n-----* and too his portrayal of Jim, the runaway slave. In school districts throughout the United States, left-wing pressure groups have demanded that *Huckleberry Finn* be thrown out of school libraries and banned from classrooms.

Ravitch says *no*. She points out, first, that *Huckleberry Finn* is central to modern American literature and, second, that Twain was one of the most powerful voices of his age in opposing racism and social injustice. "Teachers and students alike," she asserts, "must learn to grapple with this novel, which they cannot do unless they read it." And they must read it as Twain wrote it—not in some bowdlerized, antihistorical version which uses words like *slave* or *servant* or *hand* as substitutes for *n-----*.

Because the editors of literature anthologies are very tightly restricted by pressure-group demands, "bias" rules and "fairness" rules, they must give much of their attention to ensuring that the authors and the literary characters who appear in their anthologies include proper numbers of males, females, representatives of certain races, and representatives of certain ethnic types; this matters more than does the literary quality of the anthologized material. As a result, many great works that we have regarded as elements of our literary heritage have disappeared, quietly and inevitably, from our schools.

---

*In a perfect world ... , teachers would be so well educated that they wouldn't rely on textbooks; but in our real, imperfect world there will always be a need for textbooks to help teachers organize their courses.*

---

Censorship distorts the history curriculum by injecting political considerations into interpretations of the past, so that schoolbook "history" is twisted to accommodate the sensitivities of feminist groups, religious groups, racial groups, ethnic groups, and others. As a result, schoolbook "history" has few, if any, ideas or anecdotes or arguments that might excite students or awaken enthusiasm for learning about the past.

Surveying history texts issued in the late 1990s, Ravitch finds that their only coherent narrative is based on "cultural equivalence"—the dogma that all of the world's civilizations have been great, glorious, sophisticated and highly developed, that all of them have produced grand cultural and material achievements, and that no society has been more advanced or less advanced than any other. . . .

## Strategies for Ending This Crisis

What can be done to end this monumental crisis of distortion and censorship in schoolbooks? Ravitch makes three suggestions:

- Eliminate state-level adoption processes. Statewide adoptions provide the settings in which pressure groups can most effectively threaten publishers and corrupt the content of instructional materials. Disestablishing statewide adoptions, and allowing local educators to choose their instructional materials for themselves, would deprive pressure groups of much of their leverage and would diminish the role of politics in the shaping of schoolbooks.

- Create mechanisms for letting the public know what publishers, state agencies, and the federal government are doing to educational materials. Ravitch asserts that "The strongest protection for censorship is public ignorance" and that "we have a right to know what the authorities are censoring and to force them to bring their decisions into the open for public scrutiny." To that end, Ravitch advises that whenever "bias and sensitivity" detectives propose to delete words or phrases or stories from schoolbooks and tests, their proposals should be reviewed by sensible laymen from outside the detective force. No deletion should ever be made, Ravitch says, unless it has passed the test of common sense.

- Produce better-educated teachers who are masters of what they teach. In a perfect world, Ravitch writes, teachers would be so well educated that they wouldn't rely on textbooks; but in our real, imperfect world there will always be a need for textbooks to help teachers organize their courses. This needn't be a problem, though, if teachers know their subjects. Ravitch would rather trust well educated teachers to make judgments about what should appear in schoolbooks, instead of leaving such judgments to hidden censors and to the heavily politicized process that governs textbook-publishing in America today. She says: "We need science teachers who would refuse to buy textbooks that are laden with errors and politicization. We need teachers of English who have read widely.... We need teachers of history who will reject textbooks that are bland, boring, and misleading.... We should insist that those who teach history have actually studied it (not social studies!) in college...."

# 2

# Conservatives Are Attempting to Insert Bias Into Textbooks

*Mariah Blake*

*Mariah Blake is an editor of the* Washington Monthly.

*Conservatives in Texas have succeeded in gaining great influence over the textbook adoption process. For example, the guidelines for textbook selection in Texas now include language questioning the theory of evolution and promoting the idea that America is a Christian, rather than a secular, nation. Changes in Texas textbooks are especially important because Texas is an enormous market, and changes in their selection process affects textbook content across the country.*

Don McLeroy is a balding, paunchy man with a thick broom-handle mustache who lives in a rambling two-story brick home in a suburb near Bryan, Texas. When he greeted me at the door one evening last October [2009], he was clutching a thin paperback with the skeleton of a seahorse on its cover, a primer on natural selection penned by famed evolutionary biologist Ernst Mayr. We sat down at his dining table, which was piled high with three-ring binders, and his wife, Nancy, brought us ice water in cut-crystal glasses with matching coasters. Then McLeroy cracked the book open. The margins were littered with stars, exclamation points, and hundreds of yellow Post-its that were brimming with notes scrawled in a microscopic hand. With childlike glee, McLeroy flipped through the pages and explained what he saw as the gaping holes in Darwin's theory. "I don't care what the educational political lobby and their allies on the left say," he declared at one point. "Evolution is hooey." This bled into a rant about American history. "The secular humanists may argue that we are a secular nation," McLeroy said, jabbing his finger in the air for emphasis. "But we are a Christian nation founded on Christian principles. The way I evaluate history textbooks is first I see how they cover Christianity and Israel. Then I see how they treat Ronald Reagan—he needs to get credit for saving the world from communism and for the good economy over the last twenty years because he lowered taxes."

## Ultraconservative Ideals

Views like these are relatively common in East Texas, a region that prides itself on being the buckle of the Bible Belt. But McLeroy is no ordinary citizen. The jovial creationist sits on the Texas State Board of Education, where he is one of the leaders of an activist bloc that holds enormous sway over the body's decisions. As the state goes through the once-in-a-decade process of rewriting the standards for its textbooks, the faction is using its clout to infuse them with ultraconservative ideals. Among other things, they aim to rehabilitate Joseph McCarthy, bring global-warming denial into science class, and downplay the contributions of the civil rights movement.

Battles over textbooks are nothing new, especially in Texas, where bitter skirmishes regularly erupt over everything from sex education to phonics and new math. But never before has the board's right wing wielded so much power over the writing of the state's standards. And when it comes to textbooks, what happens in Texas rarely stays in Texas. The reasons for this are economic: Texas is the nation's second-largest textbook market and one of the few biggies where the state picks what books schools can buy rather than leaving it up to the whims of local districts, which means publishers that get their books approved can count on millions of dollars in sales. As a result, the Lone Star State has outsized influence over the reading material used in classrooms nationwide, since publishers craft their standard textbooks based on the specs of the biggest buyers. As one senior industry executive told me, "Publishers will do whatever it takes to get on the Texas list."

Until recently, Texas's influence was balanced to some degree by the more-liberal pull of California, the nation's largest textbook market. But its economy is in such shambles that California has put off buying new books until at least 2014. This means that McLeroy and his ultraconservative crew have unparalleled power to shape the textbooks that children around the country read for years to come.

## Backlash

Up until the 1950s, textbooks painted American history as a steady string of triumphs, but the upheavals of the 1960s shook up old hierarchies, and beginning in the latter part of the decade, textbook publishers scrambled to rewrite their books to make more space for women and minorities. They also began delving more deeply into thorny issues, like slavery and American interventionism. As they did, a new image of America began to take shape that was not only more varied, but also far gloomier than the old one. Author Frances FitzGerald has called this chain of events "the most dramatic rewriting of history ever to take place."

This shift spurred a fierce backlash from social conservatives, and some began hunting for ways to fight back. In the 1960s, Norma and Mel Gabler, a homemaker and an oil-company clerk, discovered that Texas had a little-known citizen-review process that allowed the public to weigh in on textbook content. From their kitchen table in the tiny town of Hawkins, the couple launched a crusade to purge textbooks of what they saw as a liberal, secular, pro-evolution bias. When textbook adoptions rolled around, the Gablers would descend on school board meetings with long lists of proposed changes—at one point their aggregate "scroll of shame" was fifty-four feet long. They also began stirring up other social conservatives, and eventually came to wield breathtaking influence. By the 1980s, the board was demanding that publishers make hundreds of the Gablers' changes each cycle. These ranged from rewriting entire passages to simple fixes, such as pulling the New Deal from a timeline of significant historical events (the Gablers thought it smacked of socialism) and describing the Reagan administration's 1983 military intervention in Grenada as a "rescue" rather than an "invasion."

---

*The passing of the gavel gave the faction unprecedented power just as the board was gearing up for the once-in-a-decade process of rewriting standards for every subject.*

---

To avoid tangling with the Gablers and other citizen activists, many publishers started self-censoring or allowing the couple to weigh in on textbooks in advance. In 1984, the liberal advocacy group People for the American Way analyzed new biology textbooks presented for adoption in Texas and found that, even before the school board weighed in, three made no mention of evolution. At least two of them were later adopted in other states. This was not unusual: while publishers occasionally produced Texas editions, in most cases changes made to accommodate the state appeared in textbooks around the country—a fact that remains true to this day.

The Texas legislature finally intervened in 1995, after a particularly heated skirmish over health textbooks—among other things, the board demanded that publishers pull illustrations of techniques for breast self-examination and swap a photo of a briefcase-toting woman for one of a mother baking a cake. The adoption process was overhauled so that instead of being able to rewrite books willy-nilly, the school board worked with the Texas Education Agency, the state's department of education, to develop a set of standards. Any book that conformed and got the facts right had to be accepted, which diluted the influence of citizen activists.

## Takeover

Around this time, social conservatives decided to target seats on the school board itself. In 1994 the Texas Republican Party, which had just been taken over by the religious right, enlisted Robert Offutt, a conservative board member who was instrumental in overhauling the health textbooks, to recruit like-minded candidates to run against the board's moderate incumbents. At the same time, conservative donors began pouring tens of thousands of dollars into local school board races. Among them were Wal-Mart heir John Walton and James Leininger, a hospital-bed tycoon whose largess has been instrumental in allowing religious conservatives to take charge of the machinery of Texas politics. Conservative groups, like the Christian Coalition and the Eagle Forum, also jumped into the fray and began mobilizing voters. . . .

It took more than a decade of fits and starts, but the strategy eventually paid off. After the 2006 election, Republicans claimed ten of fifteen board seats. Seven were held by the ultra-conservatives, and one by a close ally, giving them an effective majority. . . . Then in 2007 Governor Rick Perry appointed Don McLeroy, a suburban dentist and longstanding bloc member, as board chairman. This passing of the gavel gave the faction unprecedented power just as the board was gearing up for the once-in-a-decade process of rewriting standards for every subject.

## Focusing on Social Studies

McLeroy has flexed his muscle particularly brazenly in the struggle over social studies standards. When the process began last January, the Texas Education Agency assembled a team to tackle each grade. In the case of eleventh-grade U.S. history, the group was made up of classroom teachers and history professors—that is, until McLeroy added a man named Bill Ames. Ames—a volunteer with the ultraconservative Eagle Forum and Minuteman militia member who occasionally publishes angry screeds accusing "illegal immigrant aliens" of infesting America with diseases or blasting the "environmentalist agenda to destroy America"—pushed to infuse the standards with his right-wing views and even managed to add a line requiring books to give space to conservative icons, "such as Newt Gingrich, Phyllis Schlafly and the Moral Majority," without any liberal counterweight. But for the most part, the teachers on the team refused to go along. So Ames put in a call to McLeroy, who demanded to see draft standards for every grade and then handed them over to the Texas Public Policy Foundation, a conservative think tank founded by his benefactor, James Leininger. The group combed through the papers and compiled a list of seemingly damning omissions. Among other things, its analysts claimed that the writing teams had stripped out key historical figures like George Washington and Abraham Lincoln. Pat Hardy, a Republican board member who has sat in on some of the writing-team meetings, insists this isn't true. "No one was trying to remove George Washington!" she says. "That group took very preliminary, unfinished documents and drew all kinds of wrongheaded conclusions."

Nevertheless, the allegations drummed up public outrage, and in April [2009] the board voted to stop the writing teams' work and bring in a panel of experts to guide the process going forward—"expert," in this case, meaning any person on whom two board members could agree. In keeping with the makeup of the board, three of the six people appointed were right-wing ideologues, among them Peter Marshall, a Massachusetts-based preacher who has argued that California wildfires and Hurricane Katrina were God's punishment for tolerating gays, and David Barton, former vice chairman of the Texas Republican Party. Both men are self-styled historians with no relevant academic training—Barton's only credential is a bachelor's degree in religious education from Oral Roberts University—who argue that the wall of separation between church and state is a myth. . . .

## Scrubbing American History

Barton's goal is to pack textbooks with early American documents that blend government and religion, and paint them as building blocks of our Constitution. In so doing, he aims to blur the fact that the Constitution itself cements a wall of separation between church and state. But his agenda does not stop there. He and the other conservative experts also want to scrub U.S. history of its inconvenient blemishes—if they get their way, textbooks will paint slavery as a relic of British colonialism that America struggled to cast off from day one and refer to our economic system as "ethical capitalism." They also aim to redeem Communist hunter Joseph McCarthy, a project McLeroy endorses. As he put it in a memo to one of the writing teams, "Read the latest on McCarthy—He was basically vindicated."

On the global front, Barton and company want textbooks to play up clashes with Islamic cultures, particularly where Muslims were the aggressors, and to paint them as part of an ongoing battle between the West and Muslim extremists. Barton argues, for instance, that the Barbary wars, a string of skirmishes over piracy that pitted America against Ottoman vassal states in the 1800s, were the "original war against Islamic Terrorism." What's more, the group aims to give history a pro-Republican slant—the most obvious example being their push to swap the term "democratic" for "republican" when describing our system of government. Barton, who was hired by the GOP [Grand Old Party; the Republican Party] to do outreach to black churches in the run-up to the 2004 election, has argued elsewhere that African Americans owe their civil rights almost entirely to Republicans and that, given the "atrocious" treatment blacks have gotten at the hands of Democrats, "it might be much more appropriate that ... demands for reparations were made to the Democrat Party rather than to the federal government." He is trying to shoehorn this view into textbooks, partly by shifting the focus of black history away from the civil rights era to the post-Reconstruction period, when blacks were friendlier with Republicans.

---

*"This critical thinking stuff is gobbledygook," grumbled David Bradley, an insurance salesman with no college degree, who often acts as the faction's enforcer.*

---

Barton and Peter Marshall initially tried to purge the standards of key figures of the civil rights era, such as César Chávez and Thurgood Marshall, though they were forced to back down amid a deafening public uproar. They have since resorted to a more subtle tack; while they concede that people like Martin Luther King Jr. deserve a place in history, they argue that they shouldn't be given credit for advancing the rights of minorities. As Barton put it, "Only majorities can expand political rights in America's constitutional society." Ergo, any rights people of color have were handed to them by whites—in his view, mostly white Republican men.

While the writing teams have so far made only modest concessions to the ideologue experts, the board has final say over the documents' contents, and the ultraconservative bloc has made it clear that it wants its experts' views to get prominent play—a situation the real experts find deeply unsettling. While in Texas, I paid a visit to James Kracht, a soft-spoken professor with a halo of fine white hair, who is a dean at Texas A&M University's school of education. Kracht oversaw the writing of Texas's social studies standards in the 1990s and is among the experts tapped by the board's moderates this time around. I asked him how he thought the process was going. "I have to be careful what I say," he replied, looking vaguely sheepish. "But when the door is closed and I'm by myself, I yell and scream and pound on the wall."

## Standing Up to the Experts

There has already been plenty of screaming and wall pounding in the battles over standards for other subjects. In late 2007, the English language arts writing teams, made up mostly of teachers and curriculum planners, turned in the drafts they had been laboring over for more than two years. The ultra-conservatives argued that they were too light on basics like grammar and too heavy on reading comprehension and critical thinking. "This critical-thinking stuff is gobbledygook," grumbled David Bradley, an insurance salesman with no college degree, who often acts as the faction's enforcer. At the bloc's urging, the board threw out the teams' work and hired an outside consultant to craft new standards from scratch, but the faction still wasn't satisfied; when the new drafts came in, one adherent dismissed them as "unreadable" and "mangled." In the end, they took matters into their own hands. The night before the final vote in May 2008, two members of the bloc, Gail Lowe and Barbara Cargill, met secretly and cobbled together yet another version. The documents were then slipped under their allies' hotel-room doors, and the bloc forced through a vote the following morning before the other board members even had a chance to read them. Bradley argued that the whole ordeal was necessary because the writing teams had clung to their own ideas rather than deferring to the board. "I don't think this will happen again, because they got spanked," he added.

A similar scenario played out during the battle over science standards, which reached a crescendo in early 2009. Despite the overwhelming consensus among scientists that climate change exists, the group rammed through a last-minute amendment requiring students to "analyze and evaluate different views on the existence of global warming." This, in essence, mandates the teaching of climate-change denial. What's more, they scrubbed the standards of any reference to the fact that the universe is roughly fourteen billion years old, because this timeline conflicts with biblical accounts of creation.

---

*[T]he next generation of textbooks will likely bear the fingerprints of the board's ultraconservatives. . . .*

---

McLeroy and company had also hoped to require science textbooks to address the "strengths and weaknesses" of scientific theories, including evolution. Scientists see the phrase, which was first slipped into Texas curriculum standards in the 1980s, as a back door for bringing creationism into science class. But as soon as news broke that the board was considering reviving it, letters began pouring in from scientists around the country, and science professors began turning out en masse to school board hearings. During public testimony, one biologist arrived at the podium in a Victorian-era gown, complete with a flouncy pink bustle, to remind her audience that in the 1800s religious fundamentalists rejected the germ theory of disease; it has since gained near-universal acceptance. All this fuss made the bloc's allies skittish, and when the matter finally went to the floor last March, it failed by a single vote.

But the struggle did not end there. McLeroy piped up and chided his fellow board members, saying, "Somebody's gotta stand up to [these] experts!" He and his allies then turned around and put forward a string of amendments that had much the same effect as the "strengths and weaknesses" language. Among other things, they require students to evaluate various explanations for gaps in the fossil record and weigh whether natural selection alone can account for the complexity of cells. This mirrors the core arguments of the intelligent design movement: that life is too complex to be the result of unguided evolution, and that the fossil evidence for evolution between species is flimsy. The amendments passed by a wide margin, something McLeroy counts as a coup. "Whooeey!" he told me. "We won the Grand Slam, and the Super Bowl, and the World Cup! Our science standards are light years ahead of any other state when it comes to challenging evolution!" Scientists are not so enthusiastic. My last night in Texas, I met David Hillis, a MacArthur Award-winning evolutionary biologist who advised the board on the science standards, at a soul-food restaurant in Austin. "Clearly, some board members just wanted something they could point to so they could reject science books that don't give a nod to creationism," he said, stabbing his okra with a fork. "If they are able to use those standards to reject science textbooks, they have won and science has lost."

## Power Over Textbooks

Even in deeply conservative Texas, the bloc's breathtaking hubris—coupled with allegations of vote swapping—have spurred a backlash. In May, the Texas state legislature refused to confirm McLeroy as board chair (Governor Perry replaced him with another bloc member), and, for the first time since he took office in 1998, he is facing a primary fight. His challenger, Thomas Ratliff, a lobbyist and legislative consultant whose father was the state's lieutenant governor, argues that under McLeroy's leadership the board has become a "liability" to the Republican Party. Two other members of the ultraconservative bloc are also mired in heated primary battles.

But to date few bloc members have been ousted in primaries, and even if moderates manage to peel off a few seats, by that time it will probably be too late. In mid-January [2010], the board will meet to hammer out the last details of the standards for social studies, the only remaining subject, and the final vote will be held in March, around the same time the first primary ballots are counted. This means that no matter what happens at the ballot box, the next generation of textbooks will likely bear the fingerprints of the board's ultraconservatives—which is just fine with McLeroy. "Remember Superman?" he asked me, as we sat sipping ice water in his dining room. "The never-ending battle for truth, justice, and the American way? Well, that fight is still going on. There are people out there who want to replace truth with political correctness. Instead of the American way they want multiculturalism. We plan to fight back—and, when it comes to textbooks, we have the power to do it. Sometimes it boggles my mind the kind of power we have."

# 3

# Textbooks Display a Liberal Bias and an Anti-American Slant

*Marcia Segelstein*

*Marcia Segelstein is a former producer for CBS News, a contributing editor for* Salvo, *and a writer whose work has been published in* First Things, Touchstone: A Journal of Mere Christianity, *and* BreakpointOnline.

*Textbooks suggest that America is racist and sexist, and they undermine students' pride in their country. They are also biased against conservatives. Many textbooks portray Republican President Ronald Reagan in a negative light and fail to give him credit for toppling Communism; on the other hand, they often portray Democratic President Bill Clinton in an overly positive light. Conservatives need to examine their children's history textbooks and should protest to their local boards of education if the textbooks are biased.*

Larry Schweikart is a professor of history at the University of Dayton, and best-selling author of many books, including *A Patriot's History of the United States*. His latest book is *48 Liberal Lies About American History (That You Probably Learned in School)*.

## A Negative View of America

Schweikart examined the top-selling U.S. history textbooks, along with other resources used in public schools, and found them seriously flawed. Not only were liberal lies pervasive, so was a negative view of America. As he writes in the book's introduction, modern textbooks often portray America as "a racist, sexist, imperialist regime." Good news is often omitted, while America's failings are emphasized.

[In a previous column I] discussed the findings of the Bradley Project on America's National Identity as outlined in its report, "E Pluribus Unum." Concerned that America is in danger of losing a sense of national identity, the Bradley Project calls upon educators to move away from highlighting what's wrong with America over what is right, and to promote a shared sense of American identity rather than emphasize our ethnic, racial and religious differences.

But what about the additional issue of liberal bias in textbooks?

Schweikart writes that photographs and their captions can often be good indicators of whether a history textbook has a point of view. In one of his chapters on Ronald Reagan, Schweikart shows a photo of the Reagans dancing at their inaugural. Here's his caption: "Historians always attach a caption to a picture such as this that mentions how wealthy the Reagans' supporters were, or how they ushered in a decade of greed. But all presidents have had grand inaugural balls, and the 1980s witnessed the greatest boom in the nation's economy for all groups in 60 years, thanks to 'Reaganomics.'"

So I took a look through the textbook seventh-graders at a school in my area will be using this year to study American history—*A History of the US: All the People Since 1945*, written by Joy Hakim.

Sure enough, here's the caption from that textbook under a photo of the Reagans at their inaugural celebration. "Nancy and Ronald Reagan at one of their inauguration parties, held in Washington's Air and Space Museum. A black-tie, mink, and diamond affair, it was the fanciest, most expensive inauguration in American history, costing five times more than Jimmy Carter's inaugural had."

Contrast that with the caption under a photo of the Kennedys en route to their inaugural celebration: "President Kennedy and his wife, Jackie, on their way to the inaugural ball. Her glamour nearly stole the show." (For the record, JFK [John F. Kennedy] is in white-tie.)

And what about the Clintons' inaugural celebrations? Here's how the caption reads under a photo of Bill Clinton playing the saxophone: "Newly elected President Bill Clinton plays his saxophone at one of the Inauguration Night balls. Clinton loves music, especially jazz, and is a strong supporter of music education in public schools."

Give me a break. And while such clear bias may be evident when comparing such items side-by-side, as it were, students coming across each captioned picture separately would be left with a different impression. They would have "learned" that the Reagans socialized with rich people and spent way too much money on their inaugural balls, Jackie Kennedy was glamorous, and Bill Clinton supported music in schools!

## Reagan and Communism

Lie #9 in Schweikart's book concerns the credit given to Mikhail Gorbachev for ending the Cold War, and the almost non-existent credit given to Reagan. Schweikart quotes from a textbook called *Unto a Good Land*: "Perhaps more important [than Reagan], under a new, younger leadership, the Kremlin allowed long-dormant forces of change to emerge and drive the USSR [Union of Soviet Socialist Republics] toward democracy and a market economy."

In that seventh-grade textbook children in my area will be studying this year, there is a chapter called "The End of the Cold War." In the discussion of how communism failed as a political and economic system, the *only* mention of Ronald Reagan is this sentence—in parentheses no less! "(Trying to keep up with Reagan-era military might have helped do it.)" So how and why exactly did communism end? "When the Russian people had had enough, they just threw communism out."

*[T]he Berlin Wall didn't crumble of its own accord. But our children won't learn the whole truth in school, thanks to the blatantly biased textbooks they study.*

The textbook tenth-graders will be using in another nearby school is much the same. *Glencoe World History*, by Jackson J. Spielvogel, is shocking in the credit it gives to Gorbachev for ending communism. Listen to this blatant falsehood: "When Mikhail Gorbachev came to power in the Soviet Union, the Cold War suddenly ended. His 'New Thinking'—his willingness to rethink Soviet foreign policy—led to stunning changes."

What are the actual facts which these seventh- and tenth-graders will not learn? Information from Reagan's personal diaries makes it clear that he believed communism was repressive, cruel and inhuman. Again, from his diaries, one aspect of it he found particularly repugnant was its denial of religious freedom. So he and his advisers plotted and planned for years with the goal of lifting the yoke of communism from the backs of millions of people peacefully.

What about the National Security Decision Directives the Reagan administration issued in 1982 to bankrupt the Soviet system? What about the Reagan-approved CIA [Central Intelligence Agency] plan which allowed the Soviets to "steal" high-tech equipment for their oil pipeline, equipment specially designed to fail when it went online? Talk about a story young students would find fascinating!

As Schweikart puts it: "Across the board, using American banks and bullets, money and missiles, technology and diplomacy, the United States put a full-court press on the Soviet

Union." The Soviet economy didn't just fail. The fall of communism didn't suddenly happen. And the Berlin Wall didn't crumble of its own accord. But our children won't learn the whole truth in school, thanks to the blatantly biased textbooks they study.

---

*[Y]ou might want to take a long, hard look through your children's history textbooks and then prepare for a long, hard fight with the Board of Ed.*

---

## Bill Clinton and Ken Starr

But if you really want to get incensed, read what that seventh-grade textbook says about Bill Clinton and Ken Starr. "When Whitewater didn't produce any evidence of wrong-doing, special prosecutor Ken Starr turned the investigation from one direction to another. In the process of doing that, he ignored long-cherished legal traditions—such as the privacy of lawyer-and-client confidences—with chilling power. But he did find Clinton's flaw."[1]

The textbook then sets up Clinton's eventual impeachment, and his affair with Monica Lewinsky, with this excuse: "Bill Clinton was president when we were still trying to understand new attitudes about morality and sex. Television and films were bombarding us with images that had once been seen only in private." It then lays blame at the feet of Ken Starr and the press: "In the case of President William Jefferson Clinton, the special prosecutor and the press went far beyond the bounds of good taste or legal necessity in describing the president's relations with a woman who worked in the White House. We learned details of his private life that no one wanted to know. But the dangers of a runaway prosecutor

---

1. Ken Starr's investigation revealed that Clinton had an affair with an intern, Monica Lewinsky. Clinton lied about the relationship under oath. This led to his impeachment, though he was not removed from office.

seemed less important than something the president did. When faced with disturbing accusations about his personal life, Clinton was not honest."

And trust me, those few examples are only the tip of the iceberg. The list goes on and on.

So you might want to take a long, hard look through your children's history textbooks and then prepare for a long, hard fight with the Board of Ed.

# 4

# Textbooks Are Biased in Favor of American Ethnocentrism

*James W. Loewen*

*James W. Loewen is a sociologist, historian, and author. His books include* Lies My Teacher Told Me *and* Lies Across America.

*History should combat ethnocentrism—the belief that our culture is the best in all circumstances and should be the standard by which all other countries are measured. History textbooks, however, often present America as uniquely special and wonderful. This encourages ethnocentrism. Textbooks also downplay the negative parts of American history, leaving out instances of injustice or cruelty. This practice is wrong because it misrepresents the past, and also because the failure to confront injustice in the past encourages injustice in the present.*

Perhaps the most basic reason why students need to take history/social studies is this: history is power.... History can be a weapon. Students who do *not* know their own history or how to think critically about historical assertions will be ignorant and helpless before someone who does claim to know it. Students need to be able to fight back. This line of thought is a strong motivator, especially for "have-not" students, but all students enjoy "wielding" history.

Loewen, James W., *Teaching What Really Happened: How to Avoid the Tyranny of Textbooks and Get Students Excited About Doing History*. New York: Teachers College Press. Copyright © 2009 by James W. Loewen. All rights reserved. Reproduced by permission.

# The United States Leads the World in Ethnocentrism

There are still other reasons to learn history. The past supplies models for our behavior, for example. From the sagas of Lewis and Clark, Laura Ingalls Wilder, Helen Keller, Rachel Carson, and a thousand others, students can draw inspiration, courage, and sometimes still-relevant causes. We're not talking hero worship here, however, and all of the individuals named above have their imperfections. Present them whole. Instead of suggesting heroes as models, suggest heroic actions. Typically people perform heroically at a key moment, not so heroically at other moments. Students need to do accurate history, coupled with historiography, to sort out in which ways their role models are worth following. Recognizing both the good and not so good element within historical individuals can also make it easier to accept that societies also contain the good and not so good.

History can (and should) also make us less ethnocentric. Ethnocentrism is the belief that one's own culture is the best and that other societies and cultures should be ranked highly only to the degree that they resemble ours. Every successful society manifests ethnocentrism. Swedes, for example, think their nation is the best, and with reason: Sweden has a slightly higher standard of living than the United States, and on at least one survey of happiness Swedes scored happier than the American average. But Swedes can never convince themselves that theirs is the dominant culture, dominant military, or dominant economy. Americans can—and without even being ethnocentric. After all, our GNP [gross national product, a measure of the size of the economy] is the largest, Americans spend more on our military than all other nations combined, and for years athletes in countries around the world have high-fived each other after a really good dive, or dunk, or bobsled run. They didn't learn that from their home culture, or from Sweden, but from us, the dominant culture on the planet. It is but a small step to conclude that ours is the *best* country on the planet. Hence, the United States leads the world in ethnocentrism.

---

*American exceptionalism promotes ethnocentrism. Still worse, it fosters bad history.*

---

Unfortunately, ethnocentrism is, among other things, a form of ignorance. An ethnocentric person finds it hard to learn from another culture, already knowing it to be inferior. Ethnocentrism also has a Siamese twin, arrogance; the combination has repeatedly hampered U.S. foreign policy.

History *can* make us less ethnocentric, but as usually taught in middle and high school, it has the opposite effect. That's because our textbooks are shot through with the ideology called "American exceptionalism." In 2007, Wikipedia [an online encyclopedia] offered a fine definition:

> the perception that the United States differs qualitatively from other developed nations, because of its unique origins, national credo, historical evolution, or distinctive political and religious institutions.

Wikipedia went on to note that superiority, not just difference, is almost always implied, although not necessarily.

## Uniquely Wonderful

Of course, every national story is unique. Consider Portugal: no other nation "discovered" half the globe, as Portugal's tourism board puts it. Or Namibia: no other nation in the twentieth century had three-fourths of its largest ethnic group (the Hereros) wiped out by a foreign power (Germany). But by American exceptionalism, authors of U.S. history textbooks mean not just unique, but uniquely wonderful. Consider the first paragraph of *A History of the United States* by Daniel Boorstin and Brooks Mather Kelley:

> American history is the story of a magic transformation.
> How did people from everywhere join the American family?
> How did men and women from a tired Old World, where
> people thought they knew what to expect, become wide-
> eyed explorers of a New World?

Surely that passage is meant to impart that the United States
is truly special—and in a positive way. Presumably Boorstin
and Kelley want students to be wide-eyed themselves as they
learn more about the "magic transformation" that is American
history.

---

*There is a reciprocal relationship between justice in the
present and honesty about the past.*

---

I suggest that teachers want students to be clear-eyed, not
wide-eyed, as they learn American history. American exceptionalism promotes ethnocentrism. Still worse, it fosters bad
history. To get across the claim that Americans have always
been exceptionally good, authors leave out the bad parts.
Woodrow Wilson involved us in a secret war against the
U.S.S.R. [Union of Soviet Socialist Republics], for example.
Let's leave that out. Americans committed war crimes as a
matter of policy in our war against the Philippines. Let's suppress that. Ultimately, writing a past sanitized of wrongdoing
means developing a book or a course that is both unbelievable
and boring.

Our national past is not so bad that teachers must protect
students from it. "We do not need a bodyguard of lies," points
out historian Paul Gagnon. "We can afford to present our-
selves in the totality of our acts." Textbook authors seem not
to share Gagnon's confidence. But sugarcoating the past does
not work anyway. It does not convince students that the U.S.
has done no wrong; it only persuades them that American
history is not a course worth taking seriously. . . .

## Justice and Honesty

There is a reciprocal relationship between justice in the present and honesty about the past. When the United States has achieved justice in the present regarding some past act, then Americans can face it and talk about it more openly, because we have made it right. It has become a success story. Conversely, when we find a topic that our textbooks hide or distort, probably that signifies a continuing injustice in the present. Telling the truth about the past can help us make it right from here on.

This insight hit me between the eyes as I compared American history textbooks of the 1960s and 1990s in their handling of the incarceration of Japanese Americans during World War II. In 1961, Thomas Bailey's *The American Pageant*, for example, made no mention of the internment. Five years later, it got a paragraph, telling that "this brutal precaution turned out to be unnecessary," for their loyalty "proved to be admirable." The paragraph ends, "Partial financial adjustment after the war did something to recompense these uprooted citizens. . . ."

In 1988, Congress passed the Civil Liberties Act, apologizing for the "grave injustice" and paying $20,000 to each survivor of the camps. This amount hardly sufficed to recompense more than three years of life and labor lost behind barbed wire, as well as the loss of homes and businesses, but it was more than a token. Around that time, textbooks expanded their coverage of the incident. By 2006, *Pageant* had more than doubled its paragraph, added an ironic photograph of two Japanese Americans in Boy Scout uniforms posting a notice that read "To Aliens of Enemy Nationalities," and included a boxed quote from a young Japanese American woman that told her angry reaction to the order. It also devoted the next two pages to the Japanese as "Makers of America," providing a summary of the group's entire history in the United States, including a photograph of deportees getting into a truck and another of Manzanar Camp, with lengthy captions. The last sentence in the main text treats our 1988 apology and payment of $20,000.

Because textbooks began to increase their treatment of the incarceration before 1988, historian Mark Selden suggests they may have helped to cause the 1988 apology and reparations payment. I suspect the textbooks merely reflected the change in the spirit of the times. But either way, there seems to have been an interrelationship between truth about the incarceration and justice toward its victims.

Evidence shows that our society is ready to look at many past atrocities without flinching. In 2000, for example, the exhibit of lynching photos, *Without Sanctuary*, broke all attendance records at the New York Historical Society. To be sure, lynchings are over. Americans don't do that anymore. So the lack of lynchings has become a success story and the topic is thus easier to face. Nevertheless, many visitors to the museum were surprised to learn that lynchings were not the work of a few hooded men late at night. The open daytime photos showing a white community proud to be photographed in the act startled them. Most Americans have not seen such images. Not one high school textbook on American history includes a lynching photo. . . . Surely publishers' caution is mistaken. After all, in 2003 Duluth faced [the 1920 lynching of three black circus workers], dedicating a memorial to the victims after decades of silence.

Images like the Duluth mob can help students understand that racism in the United States has not typically been the province of the few, but of the many; not just the South, but also the North. Today, too, the discrimination facing African Americans (and to a degree, other groups, such as Native Americans and Mexican Americans) does not come from a handful of extremist outcasts late at night. Leaving out lynchings, sundown towns [towns where blacks were not allowed to live or stay after sundown], and other acts of collective discrimination impoverishes students and hurts their ability to understand the present, not just the past.

History is important—even crucial. Helping students understand what happened in the past empowers them to use history as a weapon to argue for better policies in the present. Our society needs engaged citizens, including students. . . .

# 5

# Textbooks Are Biased Against Women in America

*Rae Lesser Blumberg*

*Rae Lesser Blumberg is a professor of sociology at the University of Virginia.*

*Numerous studies have shown that textbooks in the United States were biased against women in the 1960s and later. Textbooks rarely depicted women, and when they did, women were shown as passively subordinate wives and mothers, dependent on men. In the 1970s feminist activists lobbied for textbook reform, especially in Texas. As a result, the intensity of sexism in American textbooks has diminished, though men are still substantially overrepresented and sexist portrayals of women persist.*

[The earliest study of textbook bias against women occurred in 1946.] [Irvin L.] Child, [Elmer H.] Potter and [Estelle M.] Levine (1960) discovered that primary school textbooks often portrayed females rather negatively and stereotypically, e.g., as manipulative. Nothing happened. But around 1970, the "second wave women's movement" burst onto the scene. And a lot began to happen. In 1971, activist Marjorie U'Ren published a content analysis of "The Image of Woman in Textbooks" in an iconic feminist reader. She analyzed 30 of the newest textbooks adopted or recommended for use in second to sixth grade California schools. (As discussed below, textbook adoption is done at sub-national level in the U.S.; the biggest states, e.g., California and Texas, have a huge influence on what is published.)

## Girls and Women Are Underrepresented

U'Ren's 1971 findings are worth summarizing, since they map out the terrain—and preview the findings—of large numbers of studies that quickly began to follow.

She found that at least 75 percent of the main characters were male, but because stories about female characters were shorter, "the average book devotes less than 20 percent of its story space to the female sex." She also found that "many books devote only 15 percent of their illustrations to girls or women"—and that drawings showed a far higher proportion of males than photographs of street scenes.

Substantively, she found stories about girls to be duller. They are shown as subordinate to brothers or doing uninteresting things and receiving no recognition even for those accomplishments. Concerning adult women, in none of the 30 books did a mother suggest a solution to a family crisis—fathers came home and took over. In one book, Madame [Marie] Curie is depicted as a mere helpmate for her husband's projects, and in the illustration, she is shown peeping over her husband's shoulder while he engages a male colleague in serious dialogue. U'Ren also documents a picture of adult females shown in subordinate, housewife-type activities ("textbook writers seem to have reduced all females to a common denominator of cook, cleaner and seamstress")—rarely even driving cars. The only contemporary woman depicted as a professional is a young female scientist described as engaged in a project she was assigned to work on that "was not her own idea." In addition to women being shown as not receiving any public recognition, their pursuit of economic empowerment is portrayed negatively. And in almost every story intended to be humorous, the butt of the joke is a female. In contrast, boys are depicted doing all sorts of adventurous and interesting activities while males of all ages are shown as strong, with greater mental perseverance as well as moral strength.

She also discovered that "such textbook stories are quite frequently written by females," another finding that has often been replicated since then. Interestingly, however, U'Ren makes a unique allegation: she claims that textbooks written for co-education early in the 20th century present a "much more favorable picture" of active and sometimes adventurous or accomplished women than those portrayed after 1930. (She attributes this to supposed 19th century "rough frontier equality" rather than the peak years of the "first wave women's movement," however.)

Also in 1971, some analyses by professional educators began to appear, e.g., [Janice Law] Trecker's study of "Women in U.S. History High School Textbooks," which covered the most popular 1960s texts and showed an almost total omission of "women of importance." The next year [L.J.] Weitzman et al. published an article in a top-ranked sociology journal quantifying gender bias in picture books for pre-school children. From that point on, studies multiplied quickly.

---

*Newly energized feminists put pressure on both large, important states and textbook publishers to reform their ways.*

---

## Title IX Changes the Climate

In 1972, "Title IX" was passed. This was a broad proscription against sex discrimination in any U.S. government-funded education program or activity. Its most famous provisions involve opening up female participation in athletics. Title IX did not specifically prohibit gender bias in textbooks. But it *did* prohibit gender stereotypes in career counseling, or materials aimed at recruiting males and females into different careers. Specifically, institutions had to "ensure that recruitment practices, classroom treatment, assignments, facilities, career assessment tests, career counseling, and evaluations are free from sex stereotypes." Title IX never was funded at a level that would have permitted widespread enforcement of its many provisions. Nevertheless, it helped change the climate in the United States. . . .

Then, in 1974, the Women's Educational Equity Act was passed. It specifically provided funding for research and training to help schools eliminate sex bias. Hitherto, insufficient money had been a big constraint in institutionalizing a more gender-equitable approach to education.

In fact, once Title IX was passed but even before the 1974 funding bill was adopted, a strong activist/volunteer effort arose to curb gender bias in textbooks. Newly energized feminists put pressure on both large, important states and textbook publishers to reform their ways. Texas is one of the most populous states but it is generally conservative in its culture, so the efforts of Texas feminists to tackle gender bias in textbooks are all the more noteworthy.

In a telephone interview, Frances Hicks (2007) provided an insider's view. When she became involved, she was a mother of three (one in the Texas public schools) who had decided to pursue higher education. She enrolled in community college and became the president of her local chapter of NOW, the National Organization for Women. She soon became active in grassroots efforts by a coalition of feminist organizations trying to weed out bias in textbooks. Their campaign began in 1972, when the "second wave women's movement" was reaching new heights.

Hicks described what happened in 1973–4. Pressured by the campaign, the Texas State Board of Education already had responded by adopting a Proclamation, paragraph 6-2 of which called for textbooks to "present men and women participating in a variety of roles and activities, including women in leadership and other positive roles with which they are not traditionally identified. Illustrations and written material shall present goal choices and life styles for girls and women in addition to marriage and homemaking. Economical, political, social, and cultural contributions of men and women, past and present, shall be presented objectively."

---

*[Textbook-analyzing activists] also found an almost total lack of work roles for women, who were almost always portrayed as wives and mothers, and had characters that were both passive and menial.*

---

## Evidence of Bias

On September 11, 1974, the feminist groups presented their protests at hearings on textbooks held by the Texas Education Agency. This was a follow-up to their August presentation of over 400 "Bills of Particulars" written by 147 women and 3 men activists concerning textbooks being considered for adoption for the next five year period. These were forwarded to the publishers, who, by Texas law, must reply to each in writing; later hearings were to resolve these objections.

The activists had analyzed all new textbooks, covering kindergarten through twelfth grade, being considered for adoption by the Texas Education Agency. They undertook a content analysis, counting the number of males and females in illustrations, and the roles depicted for each gender. They also coded whether females were watching or doing. In addition, they cited egregious quotes from the books and analyzed each in a two-column format. Here are two brief examples, one from a Teacher's Manual for a reader and the other from a science textbook:

*Quotation from Textbook*

"It is obvious that the lovely princess would have a difficult time finding a husband; no man would want a wife who could outdo him in so many ways. Josefa is wise enough to understand . . . that her ability may prove her undoing . . ."

J. B. Lippincott Co., *Basic Reading-L,* Manual, p. 2

*Activists' Analysis*

The Teacher's Manual accepts without comment the situation that the conventional courtship relationship in this story requires both the man and the woman to deceive each other and themselves.

". . . men will have to know about nuclear power. And girls will be needed to work as stewardesses on the giant submarines."

Houghton Mifflin Co., *Serendipity,* p. 357.

O brave new man-made world, where men are men and women are girls; where men know about power and girls are "needed" as servants.

In a handout prepared for a protest before the Textbook Selection Committee on October 1, 1974, the activists noted some (now-familiar) patterns of bias:

- Their analysis revealed an average of three men or boys to every woman or girl; in some books it was 10:1 or more. Moreover, the ratio widened going from first to twelfth grades. . . .

- They also found an almost total lack of work roles for women, who were almost always portrayed as wives and mothers, and had characters that were both passive and menial.

- They wrote: "it is rare. . .to see a warm, comforting mother, but *not* rare to see a shrewish one, a confused one, or an incapable one. . . . There is also hostility toward women to be found. . . . If a story character is contemptible, ridiculous, fails in endeavor, or lacks human dignity, you can expect the character to be female.

Males make derogatory remarks about women in selection after selection. It is nearly unheard of for the reverse to be shown."

- But they also noted that books varied in levels of sexism and that some publishers already "have made changes in the direction of fairness."

(Frances Hicks continued her activism on this issue through the 1970s. She finished her Ph.D. and became an academic. In the late 1980s–early 1990s, she served on an official State of Virginia task force that examined gender bias in textbooks. By that time, she found that the problem had become institutionalized, and was being addressed by paid education professionals rather than activist volunteers.)

More generally, although textbooks are usually adopted at the state level and supplied by schools, there is more centralization than might be inferred from the fact that the U.S. has 50 states. As noted, it is the large ones that have more clout. Moreover, the textbook industry is more centralized than the states. So in order to assure sales to their main (large state) markets, publishers were willing to adopt codes and standards that, in theory, would reduce (if not eliminate) the problem of gender bias in textbooks.

Furthermore, the same activist "second wave women's movement" that brought pressure to bear on textbook publishers and their associations concomitantly lobbied the different professional associations (e.g., the American Psychological Association and the National Council for Teachers of English) to promote gender equity in a variety of ways. Consequently, in the 1970s and 1980s, [according to a 2007 essay by David Sadker and Karen Zittleman] both textbook publishers and professional associations:

issued guidelines for nonracist and nonsexist books, suggesting how to include and fairly portray different groups in the curriculum. As a result, textbooks became more balanced in their description of underrepresented groups; but problems of biased instructional material persist.

## The Pace of Progress

What about progress since then? Even though recent content analyses of textbooks that measure the proportion of materials involving women and girls find only modest rates of improvement, their indicators almost never measure *intensity*. Today, it would be exceptional to find as sexist a comment in a children's textbook as that about men=nuclear power; "girls"=stewardesses on giant submarines. This introduces the topic of "second generation" research.

By the 1990s, various "second generation" studies began to analyze the persistence (or not) of gender bias in a variety of substantive fields. Most showed modest improvements (sometimes very modest indeed). [Two] sets are reviewed here: high school history texts, both U.S. history and world history; ... and teacher training textbooks.

*History.* First, [Jeffrey] Clark et al. (2004) carried out a quantitative study that looked at six high school-level American history textbooks from each of three decades: 1960s, 1980s and 1990s. Interestingly, the first 1970s academic study of textbook bias in the U.S. covered the same subject (Trecker 1971); she had found that 1960s texts omitted almost all women of importance. Thirty-three years later, Clark et al. found fairly moderate—but statistically significant—improvements: women had been only 4.9 percent of names in indexes in the 1960s, but 12.7 percent in the 1980s and 16.3 percent in the 1990s. The study's five other indicators also showed the same mild-to-moderately positive pattern. The authors conclude that the depiction of gender has improved modestly since the 1960s. They credit the feminist movement and earlier studies (e.g., Trecker 1971; [Mary Kay Thompson] Tetrault 1986) for the gains.

Next, [Roger] Clark et al. (2005) turned to world history texts used in American high schools over the same three decades. They again chose six top texts from each decade and used six indicators. This time, four of the six indicators increased a small but statistically significant amount. For example, the proportion of women in the books' indexes increased from 3.2 percent in the 1960s to 5.9 percent in the 1980s to 10.6 percent in the 1990s. Note, however, that all rates for world history were below those for U.S. history books; in fact, the 1990s world history rate still fell below that found in 1980s American history texts, and only four of six indicators rose. Clark et al. again attribute the gains to the feminist movement and earlier studies but they add women authors as another possible reason: the only world history book with a female first author, [Elisabeth Gaynor] Ellis and [Anthony] Esler (1997), had the highest—but still moderate—scores on mentions of women. . . .

---

*All in all . . . , it appears that the* intensity *of bias is diminishing. . . .*

---

*Teacher training textbooks.* Zittleman and Sadker (2002) followed up the classic [Myra] Sadker and [David] Sadker (1980) study of gender bias in teacher training materials. (This is important because other studies show that teachers develop "gender blindness" to biased texts if they have not been given gender sensitization instruction.) The 1980 study analyzed 24 leading teacher education texts: 23/24 devoted *less than 1 percent* of their content to women's contributions or challenges and 8/24 didn't even mention the topic of sex bias. Several actually promoted gender stereotypes.

The restudy involved 23 textbooks published from 1998–2001. Using the 1980 study's evaluation methods, they found progress to be "minimal" and "disappointing." The average percentage of women-related coverage rose to 3.3 percent. The introductory texts averaged 7.3 percent, but the 16 methods books (for reading, science, mathematics and social studies) averaged only 1.3 percent. Social studies offered the most coverage (2.5 percent) and reading texts the least (0.3 percent). But despite the quantitative data showing that textbooks are far from gender-equitable, they also found that "today's textbooks are less offensive than those published more than 20 years ago."

All in all, then, it appears that the *intensity* of bias is diminishing: the most egregious and blatant examples of sexism seem to have disappeared or been muted, even though the numbers certainly have not improved dramatically. . . .

# 6

# Textbooks Are Biased In Favor of Islam

*Gary A. Tobin and Dennis R. Ybarra*

*Gary A. Tobin was the president of the Institute for Jewish & Community Research and author of* Jewish Perceptions of Anti-Semitism. *Dennis R. Ybarra is a research associate at the Institute for Jewish & Community Research.*

*Textbooks do not treat Islam in the same way as other major religions. Discussions of Hebrew scripture—and the Christian Bible as well—are usually couched in language suggesting that these texts contain stories or legends. Islamic beliefs, however, are presented as history. Textbooks should treat all beliefs consistently; either they should all be presented as legends, or they should all be presented as truth.*

The wording used to describe the content of the Hebrew scriptures in some textbooks is unusually conditional in ways not applied to the sacred writings of Christianity and especially of Islam. Most often the words "stories" or "legends" or even "tales" appear which give the reader the impression that the Jewish biblical content being described is akin to fable. The same effect is achieved by an indefinite passive voice such as "it is told that . . ." or "the Israelites are said to . . ." This approach would be less problematic if it were taken across the board in discussing other religions, but it is not. Either all religions should be framed this way or none.

## Apologists for Islam

Islam is treated with a devotional tone in some textbooks, less detached and analytical than it ought to be. Muslim beliefs are described in several instances as fact, without any clear qualifier such as "Muslims believe. . ." This is in remarkable contrast to the much more critical treatment of Judaism compared to the treatment of other major religions. In effect, many textbooks serve as apologists for Islam in a way that they do not for Christianity, Judaism, or any other major religion. No religion should be presented in history textbooks as absolute truth, either on its own or compared to any other, or they all should be. Supplemental materials go even further in their unqualified praise for all things Islamic.

A majority of textbooks use a more evenhanded approach. Phrases such as "according to the Bible . . ." or "Muslims believe that . . ." are not uncommon. "Jesus taught . . ." "according to the Gospels . . ." "the Torah states . . ." "Jewish tradition holds . . ." are some analogues typically used for most textbook discussions of Christianity and Judaism, for example, to avoid partisanship and endorsement of these religions. Some textbooks, unfortunately, tend to hold Judaism to a different standard of documented history than other religions.

The favored treatment Islam receives in textbooks extends well beyond the discussion of Muslim scripture. For example, Muslim restrictions on women's freedom are described in favorable terms in Prentice Hall's *World Cultures: A Global Mosaic* in a section entitled "Lives of Women":

> Among Muslims, traditions and customs made women subordinate to men. . . . During childhood, a girl had to obey her father. After marriage, she had to obey her husband and her husband's father. . . . In some Muslim homes, women used separate entrances and ate their meals only in the company of other women.
>
> The system gave women security. Women in Islamic societies knew that their fathers, brothers, or husbands would

protect and provide for them. Also, within their homes and with their children, many women exercised considerable influence. . . .

## Teaching About Religion

Why is it so hard to teach about religion without violating the precepts of academic rigorousness and neutrality? In many ways, the answer is obvious: religion is personal. In poll after poll, most Americans (85 percent or more) state that religion is an important part of their lives, and many say that it is very important. How we teach about religion or if we teach about it at all matters to many Americans. Since *Abington v. Schempp* disallowed Bible reading in public schools in 1963, the courts have been called upon repeatedly to mediate in cases involving the separation of church and state in public schools. Religion is personal, yet some Americans, as part of the passionate nature of their religious beliefs, want to increase its public profile. (A minority of Americans holds this desire: Only 27 percent of the American public believes that organized religion should have "more influence in this nation," preferring to their own personal religion.) Many fewer parents are likely to want to know how their children's textbooks explain the Pythagorean theorem than how they handle their family's particular religious faith. After all, the Council on Islamic Education was born of a parent's concern about how textbooks and public schools were representing Islam, as was Mel and Norma Gabler's Educational Research Analysts to change textbooks to reflect their conservative Christian values.

The teaching of religion is problematic because we have not resolved the tension between the need to present religion factually, as any other subject within the history curriculum subjected to a test of verifiability, or to present religion as those of a particular faith believe it. Our national desire to provide a broad, multicultural education reflective of the changing nature of our population brings with it our fear of offending anyone. In an attempt to resolve these tensions, publishers have been inconsistent in their approach. Many textbooks are lenient in applying verifiability tests to Muslim beliefs, while they are stringent in attempting to distinguish faith from fact when depicting Jewish beliefs. The treatment of Christian beliefs lies somewhere in between. Scholars, teachers, textbook publishers, and the public itself have succumbed to the fallacy proposed by the late Columbia University English professor Edward Said in his book, *Orientalism*. Said claimed that only those from a particular culture were qualified to write about that culture. While he was specifically referring to the supposed inability of the West to understand Islam, some who design the teaching of religion in American public schools seem to be following Said as well.

Religion is different. Many religious groups consider their beliefs an unassailable set of truths. According to Muslims, for example, the Qur'an is the direct word of God. In Muslim practice, no one, and especially a non-Muslim, may interpret or represent it. If only a Muslim can write about or review the sections on Islam in the textbooks, then it is logical that the Muslim worldview of the Qur'an will prevail. The publishers do not want to risk offending Muslims, and the states have a legal and moral obligation to teach religion in a way that does not denigrate any group.

One instructive case is Modesto, California's mandated world religions course, first introduced in 2000. The course guidelines go to great lengths to maintain impartiality. For example [according to Carrie Kilman],

> [f]or the sake of neutrality, teachers aren't allowed to share their own faith backgrounds during the semester, nor are outside speakers welcome. Every class in the district . . . follows the same scripted lesson plans. "It can almost feel prescribed," [teacher Sherry] Sheppard said, "but it prevents teachers from sliding in their own biases." Students, though, are encouraged to share their own beliefs and ask questions.

The Modesto course has been successful in producing students who [according to Kilman] "... had become more tolerant of other religions and more willing to protect the rights of people of other faiths. In their own words, students say the course broadened their views and empowered them to fight back against faith-based bullying." The key principle cited by students is the maintenance of neutrality. [As related in *Teaching Tolerance*] "'It made a big difference that teachers didn't take sides,' says [Jewish student] Edward Zeiden.... Added [Buddhist] classmate Amy Boudsady, 'It made me feel safe to share my own beliefs. I didn't feel like someone was judging me.'"

## An Unscholarly Approach

While it may seem a wise approach on the part of the publishers and the states to defer to members of a particular religious group on all matters related to that religion, the result is often an unscholarly treatise better suited to Sunday school or a madrassah than to a public school social studies classroom.

*The World* by Pearson/Scott Foresman opens its discussion of Islam by Talking about its pilgrimage requirement. "The pilgrimage, or hajj (haj), to Mecca is an essential part of Islam, the religion *revealed* to Muhammad...." [emphasis added] The direct language "revealed" is not qualified by customary critical expressions of neutrality such as "Muslim belief is ..." or "According to the Qur'an ..." which appear in most textbooks when they introduce key beliefs of world religions. In this particular case, the phrase "according to Muslim beliefs an angel visited [Muhammad]" is present in the discussion, but appears later and away from the main point. The qualifying phrase should be present at the first mention of major beliefs, giving it high priority and visibility. Otherwise, its impact is lost in the jumble of other details of belief or religious history.

In contrast, in its discussion of Judaism, *The World* uses more dispassionate language. In the caption of a picture of the Passover seder plate used by Jews it reads "foods on the seder plate are symbolic of an ancient Hebrew *story*." The word "story" places the Exodus on a par with legend. Perhaps it is—but then all religious "stories" need to be qualified as such. If this is the mode of presentation, then every reference to Jesus, Muhammad, and Moses should have qualifiers that include myth, legend, oral history, or some other language that consistently connotes "maybe it happened, maybe it did not."

---

*[T]he Muslim belief is stated as fact, while the Jewish and Christian beliefs are characterized as something less . . . verifiable?*

---

Glossary entries are often the most egregious in their un-qualified depictions of Islam. Space is at a premium and explanations and qualifiers must be brief, making it easier for them to be wrong. The wording of entries on Islam relies heavily on a devotional approach, especially compared to Christianity and Judaism. Two textbooks are especially problematic. *World History: Continuity & Change* by Holt defines the Qur'an in its glossary as the "Holy Book of Islam containing revelations *received by* Muhammad from God." [emphasis added] The direct language leaves no doubt that Muhammad's receipt of revelations is a historical fact.

As a reality check, it is helpful to compare a similar entry in the same book that pertains to a different religion. The entry for the Ten Commandments is instructive. *World History*'s definition is "Moral laws Moses *claimed to have received* from the Hebrew God Yahweh on Mount Sinai." [emphasis added] Both the Qur'an and the Ten Commandments from the Torah are of equivalent importance to each faith tradition. The Ten Commandments are central to Christianity as well. Yet the contrast in language is stark. Both the lack of any qualifier in the Qur'an definition and the particularly qualified wording for Moses, going beyond the usual "Jews believe. . ." are troublesome. That Moses "claimed to have received" the Commandments sounds as if he made the whole thing up. The lack of uniformity in standards of wording about the two religions is indicative of a kind of kid-glove treatment that characterizes some textbook writing about Muslims.

The second textbook that contains problematic glossary entries is *World Civilizations: The Global Experience*, published by Pearson Longman. The glossary entry for Muhammad reads "Muhammad Prophet of Islam; . . . *received revelations from Allah* in 610 C.E. and thereafter; . . ." In contrast, the entry for "Jesus of Nazareth" reads in part, "prophet and teacher among the Jews; *believed* by Christians to be the Messiah; . . ."

McDougal Littell's *Modern World History: Patterns of Interaction* asserts "Muhammad's teachings, which *are the revealed word of God* . . . , are found in the holy book called the Qur'an." But *Modern World History* prefaces its description of Jesus' birth and resurrection with the appropriate qualifiers: "*According to the New Testament*, Jesus of Nazareth was born around 6 to 4 B.C." "*According to Jesus' followers*, he rose from the dead. . . ." In these cases, the Muslim belief is stated as fact, while the Jewish and Christian beliefs are characterized as something less. . . verifiable?

## Consistency Is Needed

*World Cultures and Geography: Eastern Hemisphere and Europe* by McDougal Littell, presents on a single page a summary of beliefs of three major religions: Christianity, Islam, and Judaism. In a unit overview for the teacher, "Key Ideas" for the section "Birthplace of Three Religions" are summarized as follows. "Judaism, Christianity, and Islam all share common traits. Judaism is a *story* of exile. Christians *believe* that Jesus was the promised Messiah. The Qur'an is the collection of

God's *revelations* to Muhammad." [emphasis added] The description of Muslim beliefs is expressed as historical fact; the Muslim scriptures simply are revelations. As if descending on the scale of historical certainty we come to Christianity. Jesus' role is less certain; Christians believe he was the Messiah. And Judaism occupies the lowest rung, its theology reduced to a story of exile, and no more.

McGraw-Hill's *Glencoe World History* asserts archaeological evidence does not support the biblical Exodus account, a test it does not apply to the scriptures of other religions. Perhaps these are all stories and legends. Perhaps all religious histories are myths. Consistency is all that is required, a standard way of approaching religious testaments and scriptures that distinguishes faith from fact.

Other textbooks repeat the error so neatly displayed in *World Cultures and Geography*. In *The Earth and Its Peoples*, published by Houghton Mifflin, Muhammad's spiritual experience is described as follows. "During one night vigil, known to later tradition as the 'Night of Power and Excellence,' *a being whom Muhammad later understood to be the angel Gabriel (Jibra'il in Arabic) spoke to him . . .*" [emphasis added] Although the wording communicates that Muhammad *understood* it to be an angel who spoke to him, the basic sentence structure still reads declaratively "a being spoke to him." It still needs the more direct qualifier "Muslims believe . . ." that covers all the thoughts in the sentence. . . .

# 7

# Textbooks Are Not Biased in Favor of Islam

*Susan Douglass*

*Susan Douglass is a former social studies teacher and author affiliated with the Council on Islamic Education. She is an education consultant with the Prince Alaweed bin-Talal Center for Muslim Christian Understanding at Georgetown University.*

*Accusations by the Texas Board of Education that textbook publishers favor Islam over Christianity are false. Textbooks cover Christianity extensively, intertwining the discussion of Christian movements, churches, and ideas with the story of Western civilization. Other world religions receive much less coverage. However, world religion coverage is improving, and it is this improvement that critics object to. Some want Islam to be portrayed in textbooks solely as an enemy to be feared. This approach is wrong-headed and goes against the First Amendment separation of church and state principle.*

The Texas Board of Education has been misled in its textbook resolution (the resolution "accuses textbook publishers of favoring Islam over Christianity and tells them to stop it"). The allegation that textbooks favor Islam over Christianity is spurious.

## Christianity Is Covered at Length

A look at common US textbooks refutes the charge, which distorts the role of teaching about religion in US public schools. State social studies content standards require learning about the beliefs, practices, and history of major world religions, taught within constitutional guidelines for academic study of religion. Textbooks are scrutinized prior to adoption in every state.

The resolution is based on charges about Islam and Christianity. What about the other faiths? As a textbook reviewer for two decades, I assert that most textbooks are similar enough to allow generalizations about coverage of religions. A world history textbook index might contain more entries under "Islam" than "Christianity," but adding keywords like Church, clergy, monastery, cathedral, pope, Reformation, Protestant, and Bible tips the scales the other way. Textbooks cover the roots of Christianity in the history of Judaism, and Old Testament figures like Abraham and Moses. Content about early Christianity is only a fraction of overall content on this faith.

Christian history is actually treated in an exemplary manner in most history textbooks. Why? Because Christianity is thoroughly intertwined with the history of European civilization. Textbooks describe its rise in the late Roman Empire, its spread into Asia, Africa, and Europe. They narrate the Roman Catholic Church's influence in medieval Europe, and its split from the Eastern Orthodox Church. Textbooks cite cultural contributions of Christianity in learning, arts, and social life. They trace changes in the Christian tradition—intellectual movements, interactions with political and social systems— through the centuries. The books cover the role of Christianity in the Crusades, Renaissance and Reformation, Age of Exploration, Scientific Revolution, and American history.

By comparison with Christianity, coverage of other world faiths is static and limited. Judaism in the textbooks emphasizes ancient times, but fades from the story with the rise of Christianity. References to Maimonides or pogroms during the Crusades do not make up for textbooks' absence of Jewish intellectuals and contributions to European culture, or Jewish merchant communities from the Mediterranean to China. Textbooks describe Hinduism and Buddhism in ancient India. Buddhism's spread along the Silk Road extends the story, but readers find little about change over time. Textbooks show people practicing these faiths today, but the gap between ancient origins and contemporary faiths is wide. Students may conclude from this imbalance that only Christianity possessed a rich, multi-faceted tradition. The charge that Christianity is shortchanged in textbooks is based on a distorted reading of the books, meant to foster a sense of victimization among Christians.

---

*Some want to project fear of Islam onto centuries of history, reducing relations with the West to a clash of civilizations.*

---

## Teaching on World Religions Has Improved

Coverage of Islam in textbooks is similar to Hinduism, Buddhism, and Judaism in its focus on early origins rather than change over time. A book's index is affected by overuse of terms like "Islamic Empire" instead of geographic terms. This usage stems from Western academics, not textbook publishers. Terms like jihad and shari'ah present another problem. Critics want to see such complex terms defined as "good" or "bad," while scholars recognize their complexity and changing meanings over time. Historical thinking skills require differentiated views. Textbooks should not project concepts broadcast by today's extremists onto centuries of history.

Content on world religions is not new to textbooks, but texts on "non-Western" faiths were often inaccurate and inadequate. Hindu Americans have recently challenged textbook coverage on these grounds, just as historians and Muslim educators worked to improve accuracy. Textbook coverage of Islam and other religions has improved in recent years. Textbooks today reflect attention to balance in page counts, topics, images and quotes from scripture. Editors enlist reviewers and take account of First Amendment guidelines for teaching about religion.

Backlash against improvement in coverage of religions— not only Islam—now portrays coverage as too positive. Some want to project fear of Islam onto centuries of history, reducing relations with the West to a clash of civilizations. Efforts to improve accuracy are confused with proselytizing or whitewashing. Such is neither the intent nor the outcome of teaching about religions in public school.

Journalists should help Americans understand the proper role of religion in public education. The First Amendment Center has promoted understanding among Americans of diverse beliefs for decades, using a framework that offers other countries struggling with religious pluralism a model to emulate. State standards reflect national consensus that citizens should be literate about the world's religions. Political opportunism should not prevent students from learning within this American civic framework.

# 8

# Textbooks Are Biased in Favor of Evolution

*Casey Luskin*

*Casey Luskin is a staff member at the Discovery Institute and a co-founder of the Intelligent Design and Evolution Awareness (IDEA) center.*

*Darwinian evolution is a controversial theory with which many scientists disagree. But Darwin proponents refuse to allow evidence against evolution to be included in textbooks. They claim that all opposition to evolution is tied to religious creationism, and that teaching opposition would therefore violate the First Amendment separation of church and state principle. These concerns are used as a cover for censorship. Students are harmed when textbooks fail to present the full debate over evolution.*

Critical inquiry and freedom for credible dissent are vital to good science. Sadly, when it comes to biology textbooks, American high school students are learning that stubborn groupthink can suppress responsible debate.

## Teach the Debate

In recent weeks [December, 2010], the media have been buzzing over a decision by the Louisiana State Board of Elementary and Secondary Education to adopt biology textbooks. A Fox News summary read "Louisiana committee rejects calls to include debate over creationism in state-approved biology textbooks. . . ." There was one problem with the story. Leading critics of evolution in Louisiana were not asking that public schools debate creationism, or even that they teach intelligent design. Rather, they wanted schools to simply teach the scientific debate over Darwinian evolution.

The controversy began because the biology textbooks up for adoption in Louisiana teach the neo-Darwinian model as settled fact, giving students no opportunity to weigh the pros and cons and consider evidence on both sides.

One textbook under review (*Biology: Concepts and Connections*) offers this faux critical thinking exercise: "Write a paragraph briefly describing the kinds of evidence for evolution." No questions ask students to identify evidence that counters evolutionary biology, because no such evidence is presented in the text. If the modern version of Charles Darwin's theory is as solid as most scientists say, textbooks shouldn't be afraid to teach countervailing evidence as part of a comprehensive approach. Yet students hear only the prevailing view.

Is this the best way to teach science? Earlier this year a paper in the journal *Science* tried to answer that question, and found that students learn science best when they are asked "to discriminate between evidence that supports . . . or does not support" a given scientific concept. Unfortunately, the Darwin camp ignores these pedagogical findings and singles out evolution as the only topic where dissenting scientific viewpoints are not allowed.

Courts have uniformly found that creationism is a religious viewpoint and thus illegal to teach in public school science classes. By branding scientific views they dislike as "religion" or "creationism," the Darwin lobby scares educators from presenting contrary evidence or posing critical questions—a subtle but effective form of censorship.

The media fall prey to this tactic, resulting in articles that confuse those asking for scientific debate with those asking for the teaching of religion. And Darwin's defenders come off looking like heroes, not censors.

## End Censorship

Those who love the First Amendment should be outraged. In essence, the Darwin lobby is taking the separation of church and state—a good thing—and abusing it to promote censorship. But one can be a critic of neo-Darwinism without advocating creationism.

Eugene Koonin is a senior research scientist at the National Institutes of Health and no friend of creationism or intelligent design. Last year, he stated in the journal *Trends in Genetics* that breakdowns in core neo-Darwinian tenets such as the "traditional concept of the tree of life" or "natural selection is the main driving force of evolution" indicate that the modern synthesis of evolution "has crumbled, apparently, beyond repair."

Likewise, the late Phil Skell, a member of the US National Academy of Sciences, considered himself a skeptic of both intelligent design and neo-Darwinian evolution. He took issue with those who claim that "nothing in biology makes sense except in the light of evolution" because, according to Dr. Skell, in most biology research, "Darwin's theory had provided no discernible guidance, but was brought in, after the breakthroughs, as an interesting narrative gloss."

*Students are the real losers here, because they are not taught the critical thinking skills they need to evaluate questions about evolution and become good scientists.*

In a 2005 letter to an education committee in South Carolina, Skell wrote: "Evolution is an important theory and students need to know about it. But scientific journals now document many scientific problems and criticisms of evolutionary theory and students need to know about these as well."

Skell was right, and polls show that more than 75 percent of Americans agree with him. The Louisiana textbook debate reflects the public's gross dissatisfaction with the quality of evolution instruction in biology textbooks.

The Louisiana Board should be applauded for rejecting censorship and adopting the disputed textbooks despite their biased coverage of evolution. Students need to learn about the evidence supporting the evolutionary viewpoint, and the textbooks present that side of this debate. But the books themselves should not be praised because they censor from students valid scientific questions about neo-Darwinian concepts—concepts that are instead taught as unquestioned scientific fact.

Students are the real losers here, because they are not taught the critical thinking skills they need to evaluate questions about evolution and become good scientists. When we start using the First Amendment as it was intended—as a tool to increase freedom of inquiry and promote access to scientific information—then perhaps these divisive controversies will finally go away.

# 9

# Textbooks That Teach Evolution Are Not Biased

*Glenn Branch*

*Glenn Branch is the deputy director of the National Center of Science Education. He is the co-editor of* Not in Our Classrooms: Why Intelligent Design Is Wrong for Our Schools.

*The US government has ruled that teaching creationism in schools violates the principle of separation of church and state. Creationists have therefore tried to argue that non-religious objections to evolution should be included in textbooks. However, the vast majority of the scientific community agrees that these objections are not serious and not scientific. Evolution is an extremely important, well-attested scientific theory. Ideological, religious objections to the theory should not be taught in textbooks.*

Stephen Jay Gould [an eminent evolutionary biologist and author] once wrote, "Evolution is not a peripheral subject but the central organizing principle of all biological science. No one who has not read the Bible or the Bard can be considered educated in Western traditions; so no one ignorant of evolution can understand science." Yet the teaching of evolution in the public schools of the United States is under constant attack. *Voices for Evolution* [a book compiling notable statements on behalf of evolution education] is a vital part of the defense.

## Creationist Strategies

The first edition of *Voices for Evolution* was published just two years after the Supreme Court's decision in *Edwards v. Aguillard* (1987), ruling that teaching creationism in the public schools violates the Establishment Clause of the First Amendment to the Constitution of the United States. Even though the *Edwards* decision was a serious blow, creationism continued to evolve as creationists regrouped in a number of ways.

Abandoning any hope of imposing creationism in the public schools, the flagship organization of young-earth creationism [that is, creationists who believe the earth is only a few thousand years old], the Institute for Creation Research, concentrated on the development of a creationist counter establishment, complete with conferences, journals, and even a graduate school. In the same vein, the young-earth creationist ministry Answers in Genesis opened the doors of its twenty-seven-million-dollar Creation Museum in the summer of 2007.

Meanwhile, a group of creationists not so closely allied with young-earth creationism sought to repackage creationism in a way that would survive constitutional scrutiny. The result was dubbed "intelligent design" and introduced in *Of Pandas and People* (1989; second edition 1993). *Kitzmiller v. Dover* (2005), however, revealed that *Pandas* began as a creationist textbook; "creation" and its cognates had been hastily replaced with "design" and its cognates in the wake of the *Edwards* decision.

Realizing that attempts to require or allow the teaching of creationism—whether as "creation science" or "intelligent design"—are likely to be ruled unconstitutional, creationists also proposed various ways to attack evolution without mentioning any creationist alternative. To their creationist advocates, such strategies offer the promise of encouraging students to acquire or retain a belief in creationism while not running afoul of the Establishment Clause.

Such fallback creationist strategies include requiring disclaimers, oral or written, about evolution (as in Alabama in 1996); taking steps to undermine the treatment of evolution in science textbooks (as in Texas in 2003) and in state science standards (as in Kansas in 1999 and 2005); and calling for "objectivity" or "balance" or "critical analysis" in the teaching of evolution (as in Ohio in 2002)—all of which in practice are intended to instill scientifically unwarranted doubts about evolution.

---

*When creationists claim that evolution is a theory in crisis, tottering on the verge of extinction, ready for the dustbin of history, the scientific community ... is always there to tell the truth.*

---

Moreover, not all creationist resistance to the teaching of [evolution] is explicit. In a recent informal survey among members of the National Science Teachers Association (2005), a staggering 30% of respondents indicated that they experienced pressure to omit or downplay evolution and related topics in their science curriculum, while 31% indicated that they felt pressure to include nonscientific alternatives to evolution in their science classrooms.

## Evolution Is Not in Crisis

Amid the dizzying panoply of creationist activity, what is gratifyingly constant is the thoughtful, balanced, and authoritative opposition from the scientific, educational, and civil liberties communities, as well as from a considerable portion of the faith community. Organizations small and large, local, national, and international, have expressed their unflinching support for evolution education. . . .

When creationists claim that evolution is a theory in crisis, tottering on the verge of extinction, ready for the dustbin of history, the scientific community—including the most prestigious scientific organizations in the country, the National Academy of Sciences and the American Association for the Advancement of Science [AAAS]—is always there to tell the truth. "The contemporary theory of biological evolution is one of the most robust products of scientific inquiry," the AAAS observes.

When creationists claim that evolution is intrinsically anti-religious, a deadly threat to faith and morals, a goodly portion of the faith community—Catholic, Protestant, Jewish, and humanist—is always there to demonstrate that there are people of faith who regard their acceptance of evolution as compatible with, or even enriching, their religious faith, and who reject any creationist attempts to portray a rejection of evolution as essential to their faith.

And when creationists claim that it is unfair not to teach creationism along with evolution, or not to teach that evolution is in a precarious state, the rebuttal is twofold. The science education community—including the National Association of Biology Teachers and the National Science Teachers Association—is always there to explain that compromising the integrity of science education in order to cater to creationist ideology is not fair to students or teachers.

For its part, the civil liberties community—including the American Civil Liberties Union, People for the American Way, and Americans United for Separation of Church and State—is always there to insist that for the government to promote creationism or compromise the teaching of evolution to placate a creationist minority is not fair to the citizens of a republic in which a basic constitutional principle is the government's religious neutrality. . . .

# 10

# The Abstinence-Only Sex Education Curriculum Is Biased and Dangerous

*Eric Alterman and George Zornick*

*Eric Alterman is a senior fellow at the Center for American Progress and an English professor at Brooklyn College. George Zornick is a New York-based writer.*

*Sex education programs are required to promote abstinence-only guidelines in order to receive federal funds. These guidelines are ineffective. Abstinence-only programs have no effect on reducing pre-marital sex, but they do cause young people to avoid contraception, including condoms. In addition, abstinence-only programs are often riddled with misinformation and falsehood. As a result of this misguided sex education curriculum, American teens have higher rates of pregnancy and sexually transmitted diseases than teens in other Western nations.*

The current *Texas Monthly* features an extensive investigation by Katy Vine into the success of the state's sex-education program. Some of its key findings include the startling revelations that:

- Texas gets more than $4.5 million a year through Title V, a stream of federal funding for abstinence programs—more than any other state.

Eric Altermann and George Zornick, "Think Again: The Costs of Enforced Sexual Ignorance," Center for American Progress, May 8, 2008. This material was created by the Center for American Progress www.americanprogress.org. Reproduced by permission.

- The Texas Education Code, written by the state legislature, requires that classrooms give more attention to abstinence than any other approach and that they must present abstinence as the only method that is 100 percent effective at preventing pregnancy, sexually transmitted infections, HIV/AIDS, and the "emotional trauma associated with adolescent sexual activity."

- No law mandates that methods of contraception be included in sex ed classes, and condom instruction is not encouraged anywhere in the code.

- Only one of the four state-approved high school student health textbooks uses the word "condom," and that book reaches only a small percentage of the Texas market.

- "In the entire state we found two people that were involved in these programs that had degrees in health education," Texas A&M researcher, B. E. "Buzz" Pruitt said. "Two of the curricula didn't contain a single fact."

This lack of sex education is certainly taking a toll:

- Texas ranks number one in teenage births, costing taxpayers there over $1 billion a year. And 24 percent of those births are not the girl's first delivery.

- The rate of teenage births in Texas is decreasing at a slower rate than the nation at large.

- Texan teenagers say they are having sex at a higher rate than the national average (52.5 percent vs. 47 percent).

The Texas story is merely an extreme version of a phenomenon that is taking place all around America. Under current federal standards, any sex education program receiving federal funds must conform to "abstinence only" guidelines, which means mentioning contraception only to discuss its failures and teaching, among other things, that "sexual activity outside of the context of marriage is likely to have harmful psychological and physical effects."

These programs are chosen as if specifically designed not to work. One long-term evaluation of 10 state abstinence-only programs concluded, "Abstinence-only programs show little evidence of sustained (long-term) impact on attitudes and intentions. Worse, they show some negative impacts on youth's willingness to use contraception, including condoms, to prevent negative sexual health outcomes related to sexual intercourse. Importantly, only in one state did any program demonstrate short-term success in delaying the initiation of sex; none of these programs demonstrates evidence of long-term success in delaying sexual initiation among youth exposed to the programs or any evidence of success in reducing other sexual risk-taking behaviors among participants."

*While abstinence-only programs show little evidence of sustained effect on a student's sexual activities, they do reduce the use of contraception, including condoms, when sex does take place.*

Of course, these programs are less oriented toward giving teenagers reliable information about sexuality than toward indoctrinating them with conservative Christian views about sex. A single grant-making program at the Health Resources and Services Administration, federal aid to abstinence education, for instance, has doled out more than $50 million in federal grants to such organizations as Care Net Pregnancy Services of DuPage, Illinois, an evangelistic organization that exists to help women who experience unplanned or unwanted pregnancies "choose life for their unborn babies"; Door of Hope Pregnancy Care Center in Madisonville, Kentucky, an organization "committed to the belief in the sanctity of human life, primarily as it relates to the protection of the unborn"; and Bethany Crisis Pregnancy Services in Colorado

Springs, Colorado, which warns women considering abortion, "Your pregnancy ends with death. You may feel guilt and shame about your choice. You will remember taking a life."

In a larger study by the Centers for Disease Control, researchers found that although teenagers who take "virginity pledges" may wait longer to initiate sexual activity, they are more likely to enjoy oral and anal sex, and they are just as likely as other students to be infected with sexually transmitted diseases. Eighty-eight percent eventually have premarital intercourse. While abstinence-only programs show little evidence of sustained effect on a student's sexual activities, they do reduce the use of contraception, including condoms, when sex does take place.

The large-scale failure of these programs is at least partially attributable to the fact that they are purposely, indeed transparently, dishonest. Of the 13 federally funded programs studied in a minority staff report by the Committee on Government Reform, just two provided students with accurate medical and scientific information, a finding that was consistent with a U.S. Government Accountability Office study released two years later. In the rest, students learned such "facts" as:

- Half the gay male teenagers in the United States have tested positive for the AIDS virus.

- Touching a person's genitals "can result in pregnancy."

- A 43-day-old fetus is a "thinking person."

- HIV, the virus that causes AIDS, can be spread via sweat and tears.

- Condoms fail to prevent HIV transmission as often as 31 percent of the time in heterosexual intercourse. (The actual rate is less than 3 percent, according to the Centers for Disease Control.)

- Women who experience abortions "are more prone to suicide," and as many as 10 percent of them become sterile.

The right-wingers who continue to promote these programs refuse to accept that their false information is in any way responsible for increased pregnancy and STIs. According to the conservative Christians in the Family Research Council, however, the relative failure of their lessons merely indicates that even more of the same may be needed. Upon the announcement that yet another study—this one congressionally mandated and published by Mathematica Policy Research Inc. in the spring of 2007—had demonstrated the ineffectiveness of such education, the group insisted that these very same failed "programs must be intensive and long-term, so that the knowledge, attitudes, and skills needed to reject sex before marriage are constantly reinforced—particularly in the pivotal high school years."

By way of comparison, Canadian and European young people are about as active sexually as Americans, but teenage American girls are five times as likely to have a baby as French girls, seven times as likely to have an abortion, and 70 times as likely to have gonorrhea as teenage girls in the Netherlands. In addition, the incidence of HIV/AIDS among American teenagers is five times that of the same age group in Germany. Is it any wonder, therefore, that 17 states have so far chosen to forgo federal matching funds rather than submit their children to the dishonest, propagandistic programs of conservative abstinence-only ideologues toward nearly all forms of sexual activity.

As if to demonstrate where its own priorities in this area lay, in November 2006, the Bush administration nominated Dr. Eric Keroack to the post of deputy assistant secretary for population affairs, overseeing a number of Health and Human Services programs, including the Office of Family Planning and what is called "Title X," a Nixon-era program that distributes contraceptives to poor or uninsured women. A favorite guest speaker of the National Right to Life Committee, Keroack teaches that there is a physiological cause for relationship failure and sexual promiscuity that he calls "God's Super Glue," which results in a hormonal cause and effect that can be short-circuited only by sexual abstinence until marriage.

---

*[A] tiny, extremist minority in Congress is ensuring that the rate of teenage pregnancy and sexually transmitted diseases remains unnaturally high. . . .*

---

And though he enjoyed the position of full-time medical director for A Woman's Concern, a chain of Boston-area crisis pregnancy centers that regards the distribution of contraceptives as demeaning to women, he was not even a certified obstetrician-gynecologist at the time of his appointment. (Keroack resigned this post shortly after the Massachusetts Office of Medicaid announced an investigation into his private practice.)

What is perhaps most infuriating about the use and abuse of teenagers as proxies for the right's culture war against all forms of non-marital sexuality is the fact that it has little democratic support. An extensive survey by the Kaiser Family Foundation and Harvard University asked voters whether "the federal government should fund sex education programs that have 'abstaining from sexual activity' as their only purpose" or if "the money should be used to fund more comprehensive sex education programs that include information on how to obtain and use condoms and other contraceptives." The condom/contraceptive option won the day by a margin of 67 percent to 30 percent. Unsurprisingly, a similar number (65 percent) said they worried that refusing to provide teens with good information about contraception might lead to unsafe sex, while only 28 percent were more concerned that such information might encourage teens to have sex.

In other words, a tiny, extremist minority in Congress is ensuring that the rate of teenage pregnancy and sexually transmitted diseases remains unnaturally high because it prefers to cling to its ideological dicta rather than accept the facts that demonstrate the cost of its misinformation.

Sound familiar?

Kudos to Ms. Vine and the *Texas Monthly* for helping to illuminate the human side of democratic, scientific, and educational failure.

# 11

# The Abstinence-Only Sex Education Curriculum Is Effective

*Christine Kim and Robert Rector*

*Christine Kim is a Policy Analyst at the Heritage Foundation. Robert Rector is a Heritage Foundation Senior Research Fellow.*

*Teen sexual activity damages society and hurts teens' future prospects and emotional well-being. Many studies have shown that programs that focus on abstinence rather than on contraceptive use are successful in reducing teen sexual activity. Therefore, programs that encourage a permissive attitude toward teen sex as long as it is accompanied by condom use should be deemphasized. Instead, the government should put more resources into abstinence-only sex ed programs.*

Teen sexual activity remains a widespread problem confronting the nation. Each year, some 2.6 million teenagers become sexually active—a rate of 7,000 teens per day. Among high school students, nearly half report having engaged in sexual activity, and one-third are currently active.

## Abstinence Is the Best Choice

Sexual activity during teenage years poses serious health risks for youths and has long-term implications. Early sexual activity is associated with an increased risk of sexually transmitted diseases (STDs), reduced psychological and emotional well-being, lower academic achievement, teen pregnancy, and out-of-wedlock childbearing. Many of these risks are avoidable if teens choose to abstain from sexual activity. Abstinence is the surest way to avoid the risk of STDs and unwed childbearing.

Abstinence education "teaches abstinence from sexual activity outside marriage as the expected standard for all school age children" and stresses the social, psychological, and health benefits of abstinence. Abstinence programs also provide youths with valuable life and decision-making skills that lay the foundation for personal responsibility and developing healthy relationships and marriages later in life. These programs emphasize preparing young people for future-oriented goals.

Studies have shown that abstinent teens report, on average, better psychological well-being and higher educational attainment than those who are sexually active. Delaying the initiation of or reducing early sexual activity among teens can decrease their overall exposure to risks of unwed childbearing, STDs, and psycho-emotional harm. Authentic abstinence programs are therefore crucial to efforts aimed at reducing unwed childbearing and improving youth well-being. . . .

## Studies That Reported Positive Behavioral Change

Positive behavioral changes were reported in 12 studies of abstinence programs [while 4 other studies did not report significant results].

*Abstinence-only Intervention.* A 2010 study in the medical journal *Archives of Pediatrics and Adolescent Medicine*, published by the American Medical Association, concludes that an "abstinence-only intervention reduced sexual initiation" as well as recent sexual activity among a group of African-American adolescents. Two years after attending an eight-hour abstinence program, about one-third of the participants had initiated sexual activity, compared to nearly one-half of the non-participants who enrolled in a general health program. That is, the abstinence program reduced the rate of sexual initiation by one-third. Moreover, abstinence program participants who became sexually active were not less likely to use contraception.

By contrast, the study also evaluated two alternative interventions, one that only taught contraception (i.e., the "safe sex" approach) and another that contained both abstinence and contraception content (i.e., comprehensive sex education), and found that neither program delayed or reduced teen sexual activity. Furthermore, these programs, whose main emphasis is on contraception, failed to increase use among adolescents.

The study implemented a randomized controlled experiment, the gold standard for such evaluations. Six hundred sixty-two sixth- and seventh-grade African-American students participated in the experiment. These students attended four public middle schools that served low-income communities in a northeastern U.S. city. Students were randomly assigned to attend an eight-hour abstinence-only program, an eight-hour "safe sex" program that promoted contraception, an eight- or twelve-hour comprehensive sex education program that taught both abstinence and contraception, or an eight-hour general health class without any sex education content, which served as the control group.

*Reasons of the Heart.* Taught over 20 class periods by certified and program-trained health educators, the Reasons of the Heart (ROH) curriculum focuses on individual character development and teaches adolescents the benefits that are associated with abstinence until marriage.

A 2008 study evaluated the ROH curriculum's impact on adolescent sexual activity among seventh grade students in three suburban northern Virginia public schools. The researchers also collected data on a comparison group of seventh grade students in two nearby middle schools that did not participate in the program. Students in those schools instead received the state's standard family life education, which included two videos on HIV [human immunodeficiency virus]/ STD prevention and one on abstinence.

---

*The researchers found that, 18 months after the program, upper-elementary students who participated in Sex Can Wait were less likely than non-participants to report engaging in recent sexual activity.*

---

The evaluators surveyed seventh grade students in all five schools before and after the program. They found that, a year after the program, 32 (9.2 percent) of the 347 ROH students who were virgins at the initial survey had initiated sexual activity, compared with 31 (or 16.4 percent) of the 189 comparison group students. Controlling for the differences between the comparison group and ROH students, the study reported that ROH students were half as likely as comparison group students to initiate sexual activity. The evaluators concluded, "This result appears to compare favorably to the reductions in initiation achieved by some of the abstinence programs [evaluated in earlier studies]."

*Sex Can Wait.* Sex Can Wait is a three-series abstinence education program with one series for upper-elementary students, a second for middle school students, and a third for high school students. The Sex Can Wait program lasts five weeks and offers lessons on character building, important life skills, and reproductive biology.

A 2006 study evaluated the program's long-term (18-month) impact on adolescent sexual behavior. The researchers compared students who participated in Sex Can Wait to those who received their school districts' standard sex education curricula on two behavioral outcomes: overall abstinence and abstinence during the last 30 days. As the authors noted, "the study compared the effects of the Sex Can Wait curriculum to 'current practice' rather than true 'control conditions.'"

The researchers found that, 18 months after the program, upper-elementary students who participated in Sex Can Wait were less likely than non-participants to report engaging in recent sexual activity. Among middle school students, participants were also less likely than non-participants to report engaging in sexual activity ever and in the preceding month before the 18-month follow-up. Finally, among high school students, the authors found reduced levels of sexual activity in the short term but not in the 18-month follow-up.

## More Program Successes

*Heritage Keepers.* Heritage Keepers is a primary prevention abstinence program for middle school and high school students. The program offers an interactive three-year, two-level curriculum.

To assess Heritage Keepers' impact, a group of evaluators compared some 1,200 virgin students who attended schools that faithfully implemented the program to some 250 students in demographically and geographically comparable schools who did not receive the abstinence intervention. One year after the program, 14.5 percent of Heritage Keepers students had become sexually active compared with 26.5 percent of the comparison group.

Overall, Heritage Keepers students "were about one-half as likely" as comparison group students to initiate sex after adjusting for pre-program differences between the two groups. The study found similar results in subsets of African-American students, Caucasian students, boys, and girls.

*For Keeps.* A study published in 2005 evaluated the For Keeps curriculum as implemented in five urban and two suburban middle schools in the Midwest. Schools were assigned by the school districts to receive the program, which was part of a county-wide teen pregnancy prevention initiative.

Taught by outside facilitators, For Keeps was a five-day curriculum with 40-minute sessions that focused on character development and the benefits of abstinence and tried to help students understand how pregnancy and sexually transmitted diseases can impede their long-term goals. It also emphasized the psycho-emotional and economic consequences of early sexual activity. The curriculum was intended both for students who had become sexually active and for those who had not.

The evaluation collected data on all students through a pretest survey, and some 2,000 youths (about 70 percent of those who took the pretest survey) responded to a follow-up survey conducted about five months after the program ended. Among youths who engaged in any sexual behavior during the follow-up period, some who participated in For Keeps reported a reduction in "the amount of casual sex, as evidenced by fewer episodes of sex and fewer sexual partners" during the evaluation period, although program participants did not differ from non-participants in the likelihood of engaging in sexual activity during the follow-up interval.

*Best Friends.* The Best Friends (BF) program began in 1987 and operates in about 90 schools across the United States. The Best Friends curriculum is an abstinence-based character-building program for girls starting in the sixth grade and offers a variety of services such as group discussions, mentoring, and community activities. Discussion topics include friendship, love and dating, self-respect, decision making, alcohol and drug abuse, physical fitness and nutrition, and AIDS/STDs. The curriculum's predominant theme is encouraging youths to abstain from high-risk behaviors and sexual activity.

A 2005 study evaluated the District of Columbia's Best Friends program, which operated in six of the District's 20 middle schools. The study compared data on BF participants to data from the Youth Risk Behavior Surveys (YRBS) conducted for the District. When the authors of the study compared Best Friends schools to District schools that did not have the program, they found that Best Friends schools tended to be located in the more disadvantaged sections of the city and were academically comparable to or slightly worse than the District's middle schools in general.

---

*The sexual activity rate of 15-year-olds across the county dropped by a statistically significant amount [during the implementation of the Not Me, Not Now Program].*

---

Adjusting for the survey year, students' age, grade, and race and ethnicity, the study reported that Best Friends girls were nearly 6.5 times more likely to abstain from sexual activity than YRBS respondents. They were 2.4 times more likely to abstain from smoking, 8.1 times more likely to abstain from illegal drug use, and 1.9 times more likely to abstain from drinking.

*Not Me, Not Now.* Not Me, Not Now, a community-wide abstinence intervention program, targeted children ages nine through 14 in Monroe County, New York, which includes the city of Rochester. The Not Me, Not Now program devised a mass communications strategy to promote the abstinence message through paid television and radio advertising, billboards, posters distributed in schools, educational materials for parents, an interactive Web site, and educational sessions in school and community settings. The program had five objectives: raising awareness of the problem of teen pregnancy, increasing understanding of the negative consequences of teen pregnancy, developing resistance to peer pressure, promoting parent-child communication, and promoting abstinence among teens.

Not Me, Not Now was effective in reaching early teens, with some 95 percent of the target audience in the county reporting that they had seen a Not Me, Not Now ad. During the intervention period, there was a statistically significant positive shift in attitudes among pre-teens and early teens in the county.

The sexual activity rate of 15-year-olds across the county dropped by a statistically significant amount, from 46.6 percent to 31.6 percent, during this period. The pregnancy rate for girls ages 15 through 17 in Monroe County fell by a statistically significant amount, from 63.4 pregnancies per 1,000 girls to 49.5 pregnancies per 1,000. The teen pregnancy rate fell more rapidly in Monroe County than in comparison counties and upstate New York in general, and the differences in the rates of decrease were statistically significant.

## Abstinence By Choice and Other Programs

*Abstinence by Choice.* Abstinence by Choice operated in 20 schools in the Little Rock area of Arkansas. The program targeted seventh, eighth, and ninth grade students and reached about 4,000 youths each year. The curriculum included a five-day workshop with speakers, presentations, skits, videos, and an adult mentoring component.

A 2001 evaluation analyzed a sample of 329 students and found that only 5.9 percent of eighth grade girls who had participated in Abstinence by Choice a year earlier had initiated sexual activity compared with 10.2 percent of non-participants. Among eighth grade boy participants, 15.8 percent had initiated sexual activity, compared with 22.8 percent among non-participating boys. (The sexual activity rate of students in the [program was compared with the rate of sexual activity among control students in the same grade and schools prior to commencement of the program.)

*HIV Risk-Reduction Intervention.* A 1998 study evaluated a two-day abstinence-based HIV risk-reduction intervention. The program was delivered to some 200 African-American middle school students in Philadelphia. Students volunteered to participate in a weekend health promotion program, and the volunteers were then randomly assigned to an abstinence education program, a safer-sex education program, or a regular health program (the control group) delivered by trained adult and peer (high school student) facilitators.

The researchers found that, during the three-month follow-up, students in the abstinence programs were less likely to report having engaged in recent sexual activity compared with students in the control group and that they were marginally less likely to report having engaged in recent sexual activity compared to students in the safer-sex program.

Although the three groups generally did not differ in their reports of sexual activity in the preceding three months during the six-month and 12-month follow-ups, the researchers did report that, among students who had sexual experience before the intervention, those in the safer-sex group reported fewer days of sexual activity on average than students in the control group and the abstinence group reported.

*Stay SMART.* Delivered to Boys and Girls Clubs of America participants, Stay SMART integrated abstinence education with substance-use prevention and incorporated instructions on general life skills as well. The 12-session curriculum, led by Boys and Girls Club staff, used a postponement approach to early sexual activity and targeted both sexually experienced and sexually inexperienced adolescents. Participation in Boys and Girls Clubs and Stay SMART was voluntary.

A 1995 study evaluated Stay SMART'S impact on adolescent sexual behavior. The study measured the sexual attitudes and behavior of more than 200 youths who participated in Stay SMART or Stay SMART plus the boosters and compared their outcomes to some 100 youths who did not participate in Stay SMART but were still involved in the Boys and Girls Clubs. The analysis controlled for demographic and baseline characteristics to test for the program's independent effect on adolescent sexual behavior and attitudes.

The study found that, two years after the program, youths who had engaged in prior sexual activity and participated in the stand-alone Stay SMART program exhibited reduced levels of recent sexual activity compared with non-participants and, interestingly, participants in the Stay SMART-plus-boosters program as well. Among participants who were virgins prior to the program, the study did not find a statistically significant program effect.

---

*An evaluation of the Teen Aid and Sex Respect abstinence programs in three Utah school districts reported that certain groups of youths who received these programs delayed the initiation of sexual activity.*

---

*Project Taking Charge.* Project Taking Charge was a six-week abstinence curriculum delivered in home economics classes during the school year. It was designed for use in low-income communities with high rates of teen pregnancy. The curriculum contained elements on self-development; basic information about sexual biology (e.g., anatomy, physiology, and pregnancy); vocational goal-setting; family communication; and values instruction on the importance of delaying sexual activity until marriage.

The program was evaluated in Wilmington, Delaware, and West Point, Mississippi, based on a small sample of 91 adolescents. Control and experimental groups were created by randomly assigning classrooms either to receive or not to receive the program. The students were assessed immediately before and after the program and at a six-month follow-up. In the six-month follow-up, Project Taking Charge was shown to have had a statistically significant effect in increasing adolescents' knowledge of the problems associated with teen pregnancy, the problems of sexually transmitted diseases, and reproductive biology.

The program may also have delayed the onset of sexual activity among some of the participants. About 23 percent of participants who were virgins at the pretest initiated sexual activity during the follow-up interval, compared with 50 percent of the youths in the control group, although the authors urged caution in interpreting these numbers due to the small sample size.

*Teen Aid and Sex Respect.* An evaluation of the Teen Aid and Sex Respect abstinence programs in three Utah school districts reported that certain groups of youths who received these programs delayed the initiation of sexual activity. To determine the effects of the programs, students in schools with the abstinence programs were compared with students in similar control schools within the same school districts. Statistical adjustments were applied to control for any initial differences between program participants and control group students.

In the aggregate sample, the researchers did not find any differences in the rates of sexual initiation between youths who had received abstinence education and those who had not. However, analyzing a cohort of high school students who had fairly permissive attitudes, they found that program participants were one-third less likely to engage in sexual activity one year after the programs compared with non-participants (22.4 percent versus 37 percent).

Even when the researchers adjusted for students' dating and drinking behavior, religious involvement, family composition, peer pressure, and other factors, the differences between the two groups remained statistically significant. (Statistically significant changes in behavior were not found among a similar group of junior high school students.) The researchers found it notable that youths who had more permissive attitudes were "not only receptive and responsive to the abstinence message in the short run, but that some influence on behavior [was] also occurring." . . .

## Sex Ed Needs to Focus More on Abstinence

Today's young people face strong peer pressure to engage in risky behavior and must navigate media and popular culture that endorse and even glamorize permissiveness and casual sex. Alarmingly, the government implicitly supports these messages by funding programs that promote contraception and "safe-sex."

In FY [fiscal year] 2008, the U.S. Department of Health and Human Services spent $610.1 million on such programs targeting teens—at least four times what it spent on abstinence education. Regrettably, last year [2009], the Obama Administration and Congress disregarded the social scientific evidence on abstinence education and eliminated all federal funding for it. Instead, they created additional funding for comprehensive sex education. In his FY2011 budget, the President proposed to increase spending on these programs.

---

*Genuine abstinence education is therefore crucial to the physical and psycho-emotional well-being of the nation's youth.*

---

Although 80 percent of parents want schools to teach youths to abstain from sexual activity until they are in a committed adult romantic relationship nearing marriage—the core message of abstinence education—these parental values are rarely communicated in the classroom.

In the classroom, the prevailing mentality often condones teen sexual activity as long as youths use contraceptives. Abstinence is usually mentioned only in passing, if at all. Sadly, many teens who need to learn about the benefits of abstaining from sexual activity during the teenage years never hear them, and many students who choose to abstain fail to receive adequate support for their decisions.

Teen sexual activity is costly, not just for teens, but also for society. Teens who engage in sexual activity risk a host of negative outcomes including STD infection, emotional and psychological harm, lower educational attainment, and out-of-wedlock childbearing.

Genuine abstinence education is therefore crucial to the physical and psycho-emotional well-being of the nation's youth. In addition to teaching the benefits of abstaining from sexual activity until marriage, abstinence programs focus on developing character traits that prepare youths for future-oriented goals.

When considering effective prevention programs aimed at changing teen sexual behavior, lawmakers should consider *all* of the available empirical evidence and restore funding for abstinence education.

# 12

# Textbook Content Should Be Controlled By Experts

*Marie Landau*

*Marie Landau is an editorial intern at* In These Times.

*The amended state social studies curriculum mandated by the Texas State Board of Education (SBOE) is in most cases not outrageous and doesn't differ radically from other states' social studies curricula. What is disturbing is that decisions about what goes into textbooks are being made by partisans with little educational background. Citizens and educators in Texas agree that textbooks should be written by teachers and experts, not by advocates.*

Since the Texas State Board of Education (SBOE) went to work on the state social studies curriculum in January of 2009, media coverage has zeroed in on some of the more inflammatory amendments proposed by the Board: emphasizing the conservative resurgence of the '80s and '90s, placing Barry Goldwater [a long-serving Conservative senator] instead of Ed Kennedy [a long-serving Democratic senator] on a list of "significant political leaders," and including Jefferson Davis' [the President of the Confederacy] inaugural address alongside Abraham Lincoln's.

## How the Curriculum Is Developed

But for many educators, the problem isn't what is included in the curriculum, but how history is taught and how the curriculum was developed in the first place. Joyce Appleby, professor emerita of history at UCLA [University of California, Los Angeles] and co-author of the widely used *American Republic to 1877* textbook, says she expected to be horrified by the new standards. But after reading through them, she says, "Aside from a few changes, I didn't see what was so wrong with them." A self-described "left-leaning liberal," Appleby has no qualm with teaching students about Phyllis Schlafly and the National Rifle Association [NRA]. "Objection to this puzzles me. People should learn about this moment in history," she says.

Appleby does, however, take issue with Board's influence over standards. "What's offensive is the idea that history doesn't require experts," she says. "People with strong political biases are not in a position to be in charge of standards." And for the most part, Texans agree. A survey by the Texas Freedom Network, a nonprofit that organizes around religious freedom and public education, found that 72 percent of Texans think curriculum writing should be left to teachers and scholars.

Appleby doesn't think the "Texas Textbook Massacre," as *The Huffington Post* calls it, will have much impact. "It's mostly an example of 'expressive politics,'" she says.

Kirk White, a middle-school social studies teacher in Austin, Texas, says curriculum standards serve to guide, not restrict, classroom instruction. Though specific changes, like the addition or removal of a historical figure, might impact textbook content, "Nobody's stopping teachers from talking about Thomas Jefferson or Martin Luther King or Harriet Tubman," he says. A good teacher, he says, will enhance the curriculum with multiple sources.

"The new curriculum is not some backward, 1950s curriculum," White says. "The people arguing over the details, on both the left and right, are working to advance political agendas." By focusing on textbooks, people forget what most impacts students' political and cultural perspectives, he says.

"Cultural perspective really forms at home. I don't know how much impact I, as a more liberal teacher, have on a kid whose parents are conservative Christians. A textbook certainly doesn't have much."

White says that the current debate ignores the most significant component of education: "What's more important is how students develop their critical thinking skills and evaluate texts," he says.

---

*What makes the Texas curricular debate unique is not that the new standards are radically different from those in other states . . . but that the process has turned into a political circus.*

---

## A Contempt for Expertise

Yet criticism of the standards is still surging through the academic world. In April [2010], University of Texas-Austin history professor Emilio Zamora launched a letter and signature campaign denouncing the Board's amendments to the state curriculum. The letter accuses the Board of being "derelict in its duty to revise the public school curriculum" and "distorting the historical record and functioning of American society."

While Zamora thinks the SBOE amendments encourage a "very narrow, exclusivist interpretation of history," he doesn't argue for a longer list of historical figures. In fact, he thinks the debate over which people to include in the curriculum lends itself to the Board's strategy to discredit opposition and "unethically categorize criticism as mere quibbles over language." Zamora is as critical of the Board's political maneuvering as he is of the standards themselves, arguing that members have overstepped their authority.

Dan Quinn, communications director of the Texas Freedom Network, agrees that the board needs to be reined in. The curriculum review process, which should work as a check to the board's power, he says, is a "charade." "The Board appoints so-called 'experts' to review the curriculum, but two of them are evangelical Christians with no credentials in the social sciences."

What makes the Texas curricular debate unique is not that the new standards are radically different from those in other states (California's history curriculum also suggests that students study the views of Jefferson Davis), but that the process has turned into a political circus.

SBOE member Don McLeroy has publicly insisted that "multiculturalism battles the American way." And member Cynthia Dunbar, a graduate of Pat Robertson's Regents Law School, believes government officials ought to be guided by the "Word of God."

The Board takes cues from the nonprofit Educational Research Analysts (ERA), a self-proclaimed "conservative Christian organization that reviews public school textbooks submitted for adoption in Texas." Designed as a foil to the "liberal monopolies" that control educational publishing, the ERA mines textbooks for factual errors and regularly presents findings to SBOE. The organization argues that as "textbook analysts," its reviewers are not required to have any background in education, teaching or scholarship. "[C]redential mongering," they argue, "is [a] tactic to dodge inconvenient criticism."

Quinn says it is precisely the Board's "contempt for expertise" that has caused so much uproar. "If they would take a step back and leave questions of education up to educators, we wouldn't have this back and forth."

# 13

# Parents Should Have More Choice in Curriculum Content

*Andrew J. Coulson*

*Andrew J. Coulson is director of the Cato Institute's Center for Educational Freedom.*

*Conflicts over textbooks and curriculum will persist as long as US education is controlled by government. It would be more American to provide tax incentives and tuition scholarships, allowing parents to choose from a range of non-government, private schools. This would decrease tension between left and right and would be more true to democratic values.*

"Intelligent design," the notion that life on Earth was authored by a supernatural being, came up lemons last week in a Pennsylvania federal court.

Or rather, the Dover public school district's endorsement of I.D. came up against the "Lemon test" used by courts to assess church/state entanglement, and flunked.

This, obviously, is a defeat for intelligent design's adherents and a victory for proponents of evolution.

It is also a loss for America.

That's not to say that intelligent design should be incorporated into public school science classes. Judge John Jones, who presided in the case, ruled correctly that intelligent design is religion, not science.

Andrew J. Coulson, "Case Shows Need for More Freedom in Education," *Kansas City Star*, December 25, 2005. Copyright © 2005 The Kansas City Star, Mo. Reproduced by permission of the author.

The problem is that his ruling can do little to end the battle over evolution versus creationism, because it doesn't address the root cause of that battle: our monolithic government-sanctioned schools.

It's that simple. By combining a pluralistic society with a one-size-fits-all education system, we have created a perpetual conflict machine.

There is no way, within the structure of our existing system, for people to get the sort of education they want for their own children without having to force their preferences on their neighbors.

Voila. Instant conflict.

Even the First Amendment's proscription against the government establishment of religion has not prevented us from fighting over the teaching of human origins in our government schools for close to a century.

---

*By combining a pluralistic society with a one-size-fits-all education system, we have created a perpetual conflict machine.*

---

And a host of other flash points in the culture war lack even that legal arbiter to facilitate a settlement. Consider sex education, textbook and library book selection, the treatment of homosexuality, "whole language" versus phonics, etc.

But just as the root cause of the problem is simple, so is the solution. America will continue to be a pluralistic society for the foreseeable future, but we can easily reform our schools so that parents can obtain the education they value without being compelled to impose it on others. It's called parental choice.

By offering tax relief to middle-income families, and tuition scholarships to those with lower incomes, we could bring independent schooling within reach of every family.

Such a system can be designed, using tax credits for both personal use and for donations to private scholarship funds, in such a way that no government money is spent on education.

Both types of programs already exist, independently of one another, in several states. By combining and expanding them, we could eliminate virtually all of our long-running education conflicts.

There are a few common objections to this idea. Some argue that state-run schools are necessary to foster social harmony or democracy, but the falsity—and indeed the irony—of this notion should be evident from the current context.

A fair number of Americans are probably not feeling particularly harmonious in the wake of Judge Jones' ruling, and many of the other vitriolic conflicts dividing Red and Blue America are also clearly caused by the official government status of public schools.

As for being indispensable to American democracy, state-run schooling did not come along until the latter half of the 19th century, jumping—as the late economist E.G. West put it—into the saddle of an already galloping horse.

---

*Evolution has been the official government curriculum for several decades, and only a third of Americans think it is well-supported by the evidence.*

---

Others argue that some areas of knowledge are simply too important to be left to parental discretion, and that the (presumably all-wise and all-knowing) state must step in to ensure that these are taught to all children.

One cannot help feeling that this statement should be followed by a brisk clicking together of the heels.

In addition to being patently un-American, such an authoritarian approach to education is both ineffective and shortsighted.

Evolution has been the official government curriculum for several decades, and only a third of Americans think it is well-supported by the evidence. Slightly more than half adhere to the biblical creation story. So we've tried the official knowledge thing, and it doesn't work.

Would-be instructional dictators should also remember that they will not always be the ones seated in the back of the flag-adorned staff car. While today's official dogma may delight them, tomorrow's could easily appall.

Surely, in the freest country on Earth, it's time to give educational freedom a chance.

# 14

# Textbook Biases Are Indicative of Broader Educational Problems

*Sara Mayeux*

*Sara Mayeux is a writer and cultural critic whose work has appeared on* HNN, *in the* Sacramento Bee, *and on the* Atlantic *blog of Ta-Nehisi Coates.*

*History textbooks are often inaccurate and biased. However, the real problem is that classroom teachers rely on textbooks uncritically. Teachers should be sufficiently well trained that they recognize errors, and they should teach so as to de-emphasize textbooks and instead emphasize primary sources and critical thinking. Current educational practice, with its focus on testing, turns history into a list of facts, promotes too much reliance on textbook learning, and is bad for students.*

There's been some discussion on this blog [the blog of Ta-Nehisi Coates at *The Atlantic*] about the Virginia history textbook that claims that blacks fought for the Confederacy in large numbers, a Lost Cause canard that the textbook's author [Joy Masoff]—she of the notable historical classics *Oh, Yuck! The Encyclopedia of Everything Nasty* and *Oh, Yikes! History's Grossest, Wackiest Moments*—copy-pasted into her text from the website of the Sons of Confederate Veterans. As will probably surprise no one aware that Google is not an ideal drafting tool for an educational text, it turns out that mistake was only the tip of the iceberg. . . . The *Washington Post* provides a round-up of the errors identified by historians reviewing this and other Virginia textbooks. Shocking though it may be that a textbook could misdate the American entry into World War I, my favorite error is the assertion "that men in Colonial Virginia commonly wore full suits of armor." Williamsburg just got a lot more fun!

## Textbooks Matter Less Than We Think

Of course there's no excuse for this level of factual and interpretive error in a state-adopted elementary school textbook. Students should be able to expect that they can turn to their textbooks for a reasonably accurate account. Barring that, they should at least be able to expect that they can turn to their textbooks for something other than half-baked nonsense. As the head of the American Historical Association wrote a few months ago when this scandal first broke, it's distressing that our educational system apparently doesn't hold history textbooks to the fairly minimal standard of, "Don't uncritically copy what you found on the Internet."

---

*I think that those K-12 teachers entrusted with teaching history can and should fairly be expected to know things like when the U.S. entered World War I, or what the Civil War was about.*

---

All that said, I'm just not sure how much weight we should place on the Case of the Fallacious Textbook. It seems to me less of a problem in its own right than an artifact of much broader problems with K-12 education. And I'm not sure we should heap opprobrium upon the author of the textbook, either. She's not the one who decided to hire her to write textbooks, who read her draft and thought it was fit to publish, or who decided Virginia should approve her textbook for classroom use.

Textbooks probably matter less than we might imagine, even allowing that it's fairly troubling that the strange political economy of American education has essentially handed over the project of national curriculum design to Texas and California lobbyists. If students were computers into whom we were programming dates and names via the software of the textbook, then it would certainly be worrisome if the software had a bug. But the model of learning in which students arrive with empty heads into which individual facts are poured until the head is full with educatedness . . . is not, so far as I know, accepted by anyone with a passing familiarity with the findings of educational psychology.

If I were to identify what should trouble us about the Case of the Fallacious Textbook, it would not be the list of errors but rather the following quote from the *Post* article, given by a spokesman for the Virginia Department of Education:

"Teachers are not reading textbooks front to back, and they're not in a position to identify the kinds of errors that historians could identify," Pyle said.

## Teachers, Not Textbooks Are the Problem

Now, I appreciate that K-12 classroom teachers can't be fairly expected to have the expertise of professional historians. But I think that those K-12 teachers entrusted with teaching history can and should fairly be expected to know things like when the U.S. entered World War I, or what the Civil War was about. Theoretically it should be possible to issue students a textbook riddled with factual errors because, while that would certainly not be ideal, theoretically that's why we have teachers rather than simply mailing each child the book: to supplement the textbook with richer primary and secondary sources, to identify any basic errors in the textbook, to explain to the students that textbooks like all accounts of history are written by individuals operating under particular blind spots and market pressures and constraints and biases, that textbooks are not neutral or undisputable, etc., etc. (to the extent and in the way appropriate for the students' age level).

If teachers don't feel comfortable doing those things, either because they lack the background in history to identify a textbook's flaws or because they don't have the time and resources and support needed to plan engaging lessons or because they feel they must direct all of their and their students' energies to standardized test prep or whatever other reason, then that exposes deeper issues in how we train, educate, encourage, and incentivize teachers in our society; it's not really the textbook that is the root of the problem. And the truth is, any textbook—even one without the sorts of unacceptable fallacies or strings of factual errors most likely to be exposed by watchdogs—is going to have proofreading errors in a timeline, to make debatable claims, to overlook some dimension of the story, to leave out some perspective—so we need to get to the root of the problem if we really care about giving our children meaningful encounters with history throughout their K-12 years (which we may not, of course, though I hope that's not true). It's not about purging our classrooms of pages that contain mistakes but about realigning all of the structural incentives that would allow such pages to get into the classroom unchallenged in the first place....

---

*Sam Wineburg, who studies history teaching, has reported that historians tend to rate textbooks as the least trustworthy sources while students tend to rate them as the most trustworthy.*

---

## Good Teachers Downplay Textbooks

I wanted to expand a bit on my assertion that textbooks probably matter less than we might think. Here's why: I'd imagine that classroom teachers vary widely in how much they rely on the textbook, and that students vary even more widely in how much they actually use the textbook. At either end of the spectrum the textbook itself is going to be epiphenomenal to whatever students are or aren't learning.

Some K-12 teachers will treat the teaching of history simply as a weekly exercise in filling out a worksheet about some number of pages from the text. That approach to teaching history is likely to engage no one, and thus I am not losing sleep over the possibility that students will long remember much of what they learned thereby, fallacious or otherwise. And incidentally, that approach to teaching history at the K-12 level is probably at least partly to blame for the fact that college history professors often report a mismatch between their expectations and those of their students. When Indiana University's history faculty embarked upon a study of their students' performance in history courses, they found that students "may view the textbook as the central source from which all factual answers for the exam emanate, while professors often conceive of textbooks as secondary tools providing students with a general (sometimes uncritical) narrative that must be compared to more scholarly writings, course lectures, and documentary sources." Sam Wineburg, who studies history teaching, has reported that historians tend to rate textbooks as the least trustworthy sources while students tend to rate them as the most trustworthy.

Other K-12 teachers will introduce primary sources, literature, film, paintings, and material culture to the classroom; will plan field trips, imaginative exercises, and debates; will model for students how to construct their own understanding of history, using the textbook as a backup reference source, not as a state-sanctioned repository of History Itself. That approach to teaching history is one that I and probably most people who study history like better, and one that I like to think is more likely to spark at least some students' lifelong interest in the subject. And it's one that mitigates the fallout of a bad textbook. I fear that every current trend in American education—the emphasis on standardized testing, the expanded scheduling of rote reading and math instruction at the expense of other subjects, the skittish avoidance of any curricular unit that might be deemed "controversial" (defining "controversial," of course, as "might make someone uncomfortable," which is what history at its best is supposed to do), the preference for watered-down, "age-appropriate" texts rather than rich and complicated original documents, the devaluation of advanced degrees or continuing education for teachers in the subjects they teach, etc.—is pushing away from this model.

---

*I find it tragic that we've created an education system in which [the] teacher is ... limited to soundbites.*

---

But I don't know for sure, and would be delighted to be proven wrong. I admittedly don't spend much time interacting with K-12 teachers, and I think our national discussion about education is generally woefully unsolicitous of the actual experiences and concerns of actual teachers. . . . What I've gleaned from the media does not make me optimistic, though of course, the media has biases of its own.

## Testing and Textbooks

On that note, I would like to close this . . . with a particularly heartbreaking story that I read in *The New York Times* last year. The article was ostensibly about how immigrant students are often segregated into separate classes within their schools, which in its own right is a development we could have any number of interesting discussions about. But between the lines, the article, I thought, was better read as a case study in how thoroughly standardized testing has colonized American education. A major reason why students for whom English isn't a first language tend to be shunted off into separate classes is because school administrators are so terrified that these students will do poorly on their standardized exams and bring down the school's No Child Left Behind [the nation-wide educational standards program which mandates testing] ratings. Thus, in the words of the *Times* reporter, these students must be "relentlessly drilled and tutored on material that appears on state tests." And if you're curious about what exactly that looks like, the reporter also provides a telling image:

> "Write this down," she told a class one day. "There's always a question about Huguenots."

> Significant historical episodes are often reduced to little more than sound bites. "You don't really need to know anything more about the Battle of Britain, except that it was an air strike," Ms. Cain told one class. "If you see a question about the Battle of Britain on the test, look for an answer that refers to air strikes."

I try not to think about this story too much, because the thought that all around the country today and every day there are classroom teachers telling their students versions of "You don't really need to know anything more about the Battle of Britain" is fairly terrifying to me. For what it's worth, I don't blame Ms. Cain any more than I blame the author of the Terrible Textbook [the Virginia history textbook criticized for its factual errors]—I imagine that she cares about her students but is under any number of informal and formal pressures to produce passing test scores. As someone who knows that history can open up new worlds and as someone who knows that 15-year-olds, and especially 15-year-olds who may be poor or marginalized or stigmatized in their day-to-day lives, are among those most desperately in need of doors to new worlds, I find it tragic that we've created an education system in which this teacher is instead limited to soundbites. I do not think we should pretend that what is being taught in this story is history.

It's funny because back when this article came out, some person named Sara Mayeux [the author of this viewpoint] wrote a bitterly dashed-off letter to the editor in response:

> No wonder dropout rates are high. It appears that the test-ocracy that runs our schools has turned even the most vital, engaging stories of human history into an exercise akin to memorizing phone books.

> If I were still in high school, I might find something better to do with my time, too.

# Organizations to Contact

*The editors have compiled the following list of organizations concerned with the issues debated in this book. The descriptions are derived from materials provided by the organizations. All have publications or information available for interested readers. The list was compiled on the date of publication of the present volume; names; addresses, phone and fax numbers, and e-mail and Internet addresses may change. Be aware that many organizations take several weeks or longer to respond to inquiries, so allow as much time as possible.*

**American Civil Liberties Union**
125 Broad Street, New York, NY   10004
(212) 549-2627
website: www.aclu.org

Founded in 1920, The American Civil Liberties Union is dedicated to defending the constitutional rights of all Americans, in court and in legislatures. Their publications, legal briefs, legislative testimony, and other materials provide a useful source of information on a wide variety of issues and cases involving public education. They have been active in fighting against what they see as the effort to introduce religion and bias into textbooks, and their website includes articles such as, "The Fight Continues Against Texas Textbook Standards."

**The Discovery Institute Center for Science and Culture**
1511 Third Ave Suite 808, Seattle, WA   98101
(206) 292-0401 • fax: (206) 682-5320
website: www.discovery.org/csc

The Discovery Institute is a think tank with a number of political interests, but it is best known for its advocacy of Intelligent Design, through its Center for Science and Culture (CSC). Founded in 1996, the CSC issues papers, provides fellowships, and lobbies for inclusion of the intelligent design theory in science classes. They also produce a number of educational materials, including documentary videos.

### Freedom from Religion Foundation (FFRF)

PO Box 750, Madison, WI 53701
(608) 256-8900 • fax: (608) 204-0422
website: http://ffrf.org

One of the leading atheist organizations, the FFRF publishes books and articles promoting the rights of atheists and the strict separation of church and state. Other activities include lobbying and challenging certain laws, such as President George W. Bush's faith-based initiatives, in court. They publish *Freethought Today*, a magazine that appears ten times a year. They also run Freethought Radio, a weekly radio program that can be heard on Air America. Archives of Freethought Radio, including shows on school prayer and creationism, can be accessed on the website.

### The Heritage Foundation

214 Massachusetts Ave., NE, Washington, DC 20002-4999
(202) 546-4400 • fax: (202) 546-8328
e-mail: info@heritage.org
website: www.heritage.org

The Heritage Foundation is a conservative public policy organization dedicated to promoting policies that align with the principles of free enterprise, limited government, individual freedom, traditional American values, and a strong national defense. The Heritage Foundation believes that good governance at the state level and empowering parents to choose the right school for their children are the best methods for improving education in the United States. The foundation's website provides topical articles on these and other issues.

### National Abstinence Education Association (NAEA)

1701 Pennsylvania Avenue, NW Suite 300
Washington, DC 20006

(202) 248-5420 • fax: (866) 935-4850
e-mail: info@theNAEA.org
website: www.abstinenceassociation.org

The NAEA exists to serve, support and represent individuals and organizations in the practice of abstinence education. The organization works to promote abstinence education through state and federal advocacy, providing effective talking points and research expertise to the abstinence community, and by providing member support and professional development services. The organization's website includes press releases, research reports, action alerts, and other materials.

**National Center for Science Education (NCSE)**
420 40th Street Suite 2, Oakland, CA   94609-2509
(510) 601-7203 • fax: (510) 601-7204
e-mail: ncseoffice@ncse.com
website: www.ncseweb.org

The NCSE is dedicated to defending the teaching of evolution in the public schools. It acts as a clearinghouse for teaching materials on evolution, monitors anti-evolutionary groups and activities, and provides advice and help to teachers, students, school board members, and others fighting attempts to put creationism and intelligent design in the classroom.

**Parents and Students for Academic Freedom (PSAF)**
4401 Wilshire Blvd, 4th Floor, Los Angeles, CA   90010
(888) 527-3321
e-mail: Sara@StudentsforAcademicFreedom.org
website: www.psaf.org

Dedicated to promoting fair treatment of issues in the classroom, PSAF generally opposes what it perceives as left wing indoctrination. It monitors schools for one-sided discussion of controversial issues, the introduction of issues into classes on unrelated subjects, and similar attempts to substitute indoctrination for education. Its website includes news on student activism, lists of books considered inflammatory or one-sided, and other resources for students, teachers, and community members.

## Planned Parenthood

810 Seventh Ave., New York, NY  10019
(212) 541-7800 • fax: (212) 245-1845

Planned Parenthood is a national organization that supports people's right to make their own reproductive decisions without governmental interference. It provides contraceptive counseling and services at clinics located throughout the United States. Its website includes numerous publications and articles, including many focusing on sex education and the problems with abstinence-only curricula.

## The Textbook League (TTL)

PMB 272, 40 Fourth Street, Petaluma, California  94952
e-mail: ttl@textbookleague.org
website: www.textbookleague.org

The textbook league is an organization dedicated to supporting the creation and acceptance of sound textbooks. It publishes *The Textbook Letter*. The TTL website includes most issues of *The Textbook Letter*, as well as additional online articles evaluating and discussing textbooks.

## United States Department of Education (ED)

400 Maryland Ave., SW, Washington, DC  20202
(800) 872-5327
website: www.ed.gov

ED was established by Congress on May 4, 1980, with the goal of improving education nationwide through the use of federally mandated education programs. Initiatives by ED have focused on increasing the accountability of public schools and teachers, as well as providing research and evaluation on school issues. ED publishes a variety of newsletters on specific topics relating to education; all of these and other publications and reports by the department can be accessed online.

# Bibliography

## Books

| | |
|---|---|
| Michael Apple and Linda Christian-Smith, eds. | *The Politics of the Textbook*. New York: Routledge, 1991. |
| Steve Baldwin and Karen Holgate | *From Crayons to Condoms: The Ugly Truth About America's Public Schools*. Los Angeles: WND Books, 2008. |
| William A. Dembski and Jonathan Witt | *Intelligent Design Uncensored: An Easy-to-Understand Guide to the Controversy*. Downers Grove, IL: InterVarsity Press, 2010. |
| Ronald W. Evans | *The Social Studies Wars: What Should We Teach the Children?* New York: Teachers College Press, 2004. |
| David Horowitz | *One-Party Classroom: How Radical Professors at America's Top Colleges Indoctrinate Students and Undermine Our Democracy*. New York: Crown Publishing Group, 2009. |
| Christopher R. Leahy | *Whitewashing War: Historical Myth, Corporate Textbooks, and Possibilities for Democratic Education*. New York: Teachers College Press, 2009. |

Kristin Luker — *When Sex Goes to School: Warring Views on Sex—and Sex Education—Since the Sixties.* New York: W.W. Norton & Company, 2006.

Carol Mason — *Reading Appalachia from Left to Right: Conservatives and the 1974 Kanawha County Textbook Controversy.* Ithaca, NY: Cornell University Press, 2009.

Cris Mayo — *Disputing the Subject of Sex: Sexuality and Public School Controversies.* Lanham, MD: Rowman & Littlefield Publishers, 2007.

Diane Ravitch — *The Language Police: How Pressure Groups Restrict What Students Learn.* New York: Alfred A. Knopf, 2003.

David Sadker and Karen Zittleman — *Still Failing at Fairness: How Gender Bias Cheats Girls and Boys in School and What We Can Do About It.* New York: Simon & Schuster, 2009.

Larry Schweikart — *48 Liberal Lies About American History.* New York: Penguin Group, 2008.

Eugenie C. Scott and Glenn Branch — *Not in Our Classrooms: Why Intelligent Design Is Wrong for Our Schools.* Boston: Beacon Press, 2006.

Mano Singham — *God vs. Darwin: The War Between Evolution and Creationism in the Classroom.* Lanham, MD: Rowman & Littlefield, 2009.

# Periodicals and Internet Sources

Kate Alexander — "Texas' Influence on Textbooks Could Wane," Statesman.com, March 9, 2010.

Ronald Bailey — "Creation Summer Camp," *Reason*, July 19, 2005.

Michael Dabney — "Science Textbooks Make Girls Study Harder," *Epoch Times*, September 3, 2010.

Rod Dreher — "Teaching Islam," *National Review*, February 12, 2002.

Martha Gies-Chumney — "Exclusive: Review 'The Trouble With Textbooks—Distorting History and Religion,'" *Family Security Matters*, October 8, 2009.

Danielle Glazer — "Textbook Bias Against Israel," *Accuracy in Academia*, June 1, 2005.

Trey Kay, Deborah George, and Stan Bumgardner — "The Great Textbook Wars," *American RadioWorks*, n.d. Americanradioworks.publicradio.org

James C. McKinley, Jr. — "A Claim of Pro-Islam Bias in Textbooks," *New York Times*, September 22, 2010.

Carie McLaren — "A Conversation with Historian and Author James Loewen. Sort Of." *Stay Free!*, 18, Spring 2001.

Elizabeth O'Brien    "Major Study Reveals Overwhelming Bias of 'Comprehensive' Sex Education," *LifeSiteNews*, June 18, 2007.

Susan Orr    "Holding the Sex Educators Accountable," *The Family in America: A Journal of Public Policy*, Summer 2010.

Diane Ravitch    "'T' Is for 'Texas Textbook,'" *Daily Beast*, March 14, 2010.

Erik Robelen    "Textbook Battle Brewing in Louisiana Over Evolution," *Education Week*, November 12, 2010.

David Roemer    "Book Review. Only a Theory: Evolution and the Battle for America's Soul," OrthodoxyToday.org, 2008.

David Sadker    "Seven Forms of Bias in Instructional Materials," *Myra Sadker Foundation Website*, n.d. www.sadker.org

Sex and Censorship Committee, National Coalition Against Censorship    "Abstinence-Only 'Sex' Education," Planned Parenthood Affiliates New Jersey, October 22, 2007.

Tom Shuford    "Political Correctness in Textbooks," North Carolina Education Alliance, May 25, 2004.

Kevin Sieff      "Virginia 4th-Grade Textbook Criticized Over Claims on Black Confederate Soldiers," *Washington Post*, October 20, 2010.

Rob Weir      "Teaching Without Textbooks," *Inside Higher Ed*, March 6. 2007.

Pamela R. Winnick      "A Textbook Case of Junk Science," WeeklyStandard.com, May 9, 2005.

# Index

## A

Abstinence-only sex education. *See* Sex education
*Adventures of Huckleberry Finn* (Twain), 19–20
African Americans, 29–30, 46–47, 86–87
Age stereotypes, 16
Alterman, Eric, 78
American history. *See* History textbooks
*The American Pageant* (Bailey), 45
American Way, 26
Ames, Bill, 28
Anthologies, 20
Appleby, Joyce, 98–99
*The Autobiography of Malcolm X* (Malcolm X), 7

## B

Barton, David, 28–30
Best Friends program, 90–91
Biology textbooks. *See* Science textbooks
Blake, Marian, 23
Blandness, 16–17
Blumberg, Rae Lesser, 48
Boorstin, Daniel, 43
Boys and Girls Club, 93
Bradley Project, 36
Branch, Glenn, 74

## C

California, 48–49
Cargill, Barbara, 31

Carter, Jimmy, 37
Censorship, 10–17, 72–73
Character-building programs, 90
Christianity, 7–9, 59, 64–65, 66–69
Church/state separation, 75, 102–103
Citizen-review process, 25–26
Civil Liberties Act, 45
Civil liberties organizations, 77
Clendenin, Richard, 8
Climate change, 32
Clinton, Bill, 12, 37, 39–40
Cold War, ending of the, 37–39
Conservatives
    citizen-review process, 25–26
    Educational Research Analysts, 101
    right-wing pressure groups, 18
    Texas, 24–25, 27–31, 33–34
Constitution, U.S., 29
Contraception, 81, 87, 96
Coulson, Andrew J., 102
Creationism, 32–33, 72, 75–76, 102–103
Cultural equivalence, 20–21
Curriculum standards, 31–33, 99–101, 103–105

## D

Darwinism. *See* Evolution
Discrimination, racial, 46–47
District of Columbia, 90–91
Douglass, Susan, 66
Dover Public School District, 102–103

# E

Economic issues, 24–25
Education community, 77
Educational Research Analysts, 101
Educators. *See* Teachers
English as a second language,
 111–112
English curriculum standards, 31
Ethnocentrism, 41–47
Evolution, 23–25
 biology textbooks, 70–73
 Gould, Stephen Jay, 74
 McLeroy, Don, 23–24
 scientific community, 76–77
 state-run schools, 105
 Texas, 26, 32–33
Exceptionalism, American, 44

# F

Fairness, representational, 16
Federal funding, 78–79, 96–97
First Amendment, 72–73, 75
FitzGerald, Frances, 25
For Keeps sex education curricu-
 lum, 89–90
*48 Liberal Lies About American
 History (That You Probably
 Learned in School)* (Schweikart),
 35

# G

Gabler, Norma and Mel, 25–26
Gagnon, Paul, 44
Gender, 59–60
Gender stereotypes, 16
*Glencoe World History*
 (Spielvogel), 38, 65
Global warming, 32

Gorbachev, Mikhail, 37–38
Gould, Stephen Jay, 74
Guidelines, publishers', 19, 54–55

# H

Hakim, Joy, 36
Harrah, Lewis, 7
Health textbooks, 26
Heritage Keepers, 89
Hicks, Frances, 51–54
Hillis, David, 33
*A History of the United States*
 (Boorstin and Kelley), 43–44
*A History of the US: All the People
 Since 1945* (Hakim), 36–37
History textbooks
 American ethnocentrism,
  41–47
 cultural equivalence, 20–21
 liberal bias, 35–40
 mistakes in, 106–108
 teachers, 108–111
 Texas, 27–31, 98–101
 women's representation in, 55
HIV Risk-Reduction Intervention,
 92–93
Horan, Marvin, 7, 9

# I

"The Image of Woman in Text-
 books" (U'Ren), 48–49
Inaugural celebrations, 36–37
Institute for Creation Research, 75
Intelligent design, 32–33, 72, 75,
 102–103
International comparisons of teen
 sexual behavior, 82

Internment, Japanese American, 45–46

Islam, 29, 58–65, 66–69

## J

Japanese American internment, 45–46

Jones, John, 102–103

Judaism, 58, 59, 63, 64–65

## K

Kanawha County, West Virginia, 7–9

Kelley, Brooks Mather, 43

Kennedy, John F., 37

Keroack, Eric, 82–83

Kim, Christine, 85

King, Martin Luther, Jr., 30

Koonin, Eugene, 72

Kracht, James, 30–31

Ku Klux Klan (KKK), 8

## L

Landau, Marie, 98

Language, use of, 10–22

Language arts curriculum standards, 31

*The Language Police* (Ravitch), 10–17, 19–22

Leftist pressure groups, 18, 19–20

Leininger, James, 28

Liberal bias, 35–40

Little Rock, Arkansas, 92

Local policies *vs.* statewide policies, 21

Loewen, James W., 41

Louisiana, 70–73

Lowe, Gail, 31

Luskin, Casey, 70

Lynchings, 46–47

## M

Marshall, Peter, 28, 30

Mayeux, Sara, 106

Mayr, Ernst, 23

McCarthy, Joseph, 29

McLeroy, Don, 23–25, 27–28, 32, 33–34, 101

Misinformation, 81–82, 106–108

Modesto, California, 61–62

Monroe County, New York, 91–92

Moore, Alice, 7, 9

## N

National Assessment Government Board (NAGB), 11–13

National Education Association (NEA), 7, 8

National Organization for Women (NOW), 51

New York Historical Society, 46

"Non-Western" faiths, 68–69

Not Me, Not Now program, 91–92

## O

Offutt, Robert, 27

## P

Parents, 103–105

*A Patriot's History of the United States* (Schweikart), 35

People for the American Way, 26

Perry, Rick, 27, 33

Philadelphia, Pennsylvania, 92–93

Politics, 27, 33–34, 99

Pressure groups, 18, 19–20
Project Taking Charge, 94
Pronouns, 16
Public awareness, 21
Public opinion, 83–84
Publishers, 19, 54–55
    self-censorship, 17–19
    Texas editions, 26

**Q**

Quinn, Dan, 100–101
Qur'an, 61, 62, 64–65

**R**

Racism, 46–47
Ratliff, Thomas, 33
Ravitch, Diane, 10–13, 19–22
Reagan, Ronald, 24, 36–39
Reasons of the Heart sex education curriculum, 87–88
Rector, Robert, 85
Religion
    Christianity, textbook coverage of, 66–69
    evolution, 77
    Islam, 58–65
    Kanawha County textbook controversy, 7–8
    religious language, 63–64
Representational fairness, 16
Republican Party, 27, 29
Right-wing pressure groups, 18

**S**

School choice, 103–105
Schweikart, Larry, 35–36, 38
Science textbooks, 26, 31–33, 70–73

Scientific community, 76–77
Segelstein, Marcia, 35
Selden, Mark, 46
Self-censorship, publisher, 17–19
Sex education
    Abstinence by Choice program, 92
    abstinence-only sex education, 78, 81–82
    African American adolescents, 86–87
    Best Friends program, 90–91
    funding, 96–97
    Heritage Keepers, 89
    HIV Risk-Reduction Intervention program, 92–93
    For Keeps sex education curriculum, 89–90
    Not Me, Not Now program, 91–92
    Project Taking Charge, 94
    Reasons of the Heart sex education curriculum, 87–88
    Sex Can Wait sex education curriculum, 88–89
    Stay SMART program, 93–94
    Teen Aid and Sex Respect program, 95
    Texas, 78–84
Sexually transmitted diseases, 82, 85–86, 92–93
Skell, Phil, 72–73
Social studies. *See* History textbooks
Soviet Union, 37–39
Spielvogel, Jackson J., 38
Standardized tests, 111–113
Starr, Ken, 39–40
State-level adoption processes, 21
State-run schools, 103–105
Sweden, 42

**T**

Teachers
    Kanawha County textbook
      controversy, 8
    reliance on textbooks, 21–22
    teacher training, 56–57
    Texas history curriculum, 98–
      101
    *vs.* textbooks, 108–111
Teen Aid and Sex Respect pro-
  gram, 95
Teen sexual activity. *See* Sex edu-
  cation
Testing, standardized, 111–113
Texas
    citizen-review process, 25–26
    curriculum standards, 31–33
    history textbooks, 27–31, 98–
      101
    politics, 33–34
    social studies curriculum,
      28–30
    textbook adoption process
      overhaul, 26–27
    textbook market, 24–25
    women's representation in
      textbooks, 51–54
Texas Education Agency, 27–28, 52
*Texas Monthly* (magazine), 78–79
Texas Public Policy Foundation,
  28
Texas State Board of Education,
  24, 30–34
Textbook Selection Committee,
  Texas, 53–54
Textbooks, 7–113
    bias in, 23–34, 35–40; 73–77
    censorship in, 15–18
    Christianity in, 66–69
    ethnocentrism in, 41–45

evolution in, 70–73
history textbooks, 35–38, 43–
  45, 56, 106, 108
Islam in, 58–65
women's representation in,
  48–52, 54–55
*The World* (Pearson/Scott
  Foresman), 62–63
*World Civilizations: The Global
  Experience* (Pearson
  Longman), 64
*World Cultures: A Global Mo-
  saic* (Prentice Hall), 59–60
*World Cultures and Geography:
  Eastern Hemisphere and Eu-
  rope* (McDougal Littell), 64
*World History: Continuity &
  Change* (Holt), 63
world religion textbooks, 60–
  62, 68–69
Title IX, 50–52
Tobin, Gary A., 58
Topics, controversial, 15–17

**U**

Ultraconservatives, 33–34
Underrepresentation of women
  and girls, 49–50
U'Ren, Marjorie, 48–49
Utah, 95

**V**

Vine, Katy, 78, 84
Violence, 7
Virginia, 87–88, 106–108

**W**

West Point, Mississippi, 94
Westwater, Anne C., 10
White, Kirk, 99–101

Whitewater investigation, 39–40

Wilmington, Delaware, 94

*Without Sanctuary* (exhibit), 46

Women

    evidence of bias, 52–55

    "The Image of Woman in
Textbooks" (U'Ren), 48–49

    Islam, 59–60

    progress in reducing gender
bias, 55–57

    Title IX, 50–52

    underrepresentation, 49–50

Women's Educational Equity Act,
51

World War II, 45–46

**Y**

Ybarra, Dennis R., 58

Youth Risk Behavior Survey,
90–91

**Z**

Zamora, Emilio, 100

Zornick, George, 78